MW01252046

Constructing The Narrative
In Super-vision

for all those colleagues
who have participated with me
in super-vision relationships

Constructing The Narrative
In Super-vision

Johnella Bird

Edge Press

www.heartsnarrative.cc
edgepress@xtra.co.nz

PO Box 80089 Green Bay
Auckland 0643 New Zealand

ISBN-13: 978-0-473-11446-6
ISBN-10: 0-473-11446-1

The right of Johnella Bird to be identified as the author of this work
in terms of Section 96 of the Copyright Act 1994 is here asserted.
Johnella Bird, 2006

Other titles by Johnella Bird

**The Heart's Narrative: Therapy and
Navigating Life's Contradictions (2000)**

**Talk that Sings: Therapy in a
New Linguistic Key (2004)**

All rights reserved. Without limiting the rights under copyright reserved
above, no part of this publication may be reproduced, stored in or introduced
into a retrieval system, or transmitted, in any form or by any means (electronic,
mechanical, photocopying, recording or otherwise), without the prior written
permission of both the copyright owner and the above publisher of this book.

cover design Secret Life Media
text design and typeset Susan Corby Design
editorial assistance Pat Rosier, Leela Anderson
printing Publishing Press Limited, Auckland

contents

introduction   vii

1 introducing prismatic dialogue   1

stepping through the prismatic dialogue process
escaping binary oppositions
preparing to listen to the tape
post interview follow up
common dilemmas
prismatic dialogue and time
the benefits of prismatic dialogue
extra-vision through prismatic dialogue
extending the clinical edge of the counsellor

2 super-vision and experiential knowledge   35

introducing possibilities through using tentative language
re-searching experience by taking up the inside/outside position

3 prioritising the therapist   55

the boundary that surrounds the professional and the personal
reconnecting with feelings and experiences
prioritising relational presence through super-vision

**4 the power relation in super-vision
and consultation relationships**   75

accountability through relational consciousness
exposing the operation of power

5 extending the imaginative resource   97

common questions asked in super-vision

conclusion   109

notes   111

references   117

appendix 1   121

appendix 2   131

introduction

People often take up the role of 'supervisor' when they or others deem them to be ready or proficient enough for this responsibility. I began my career as a 'supervisor' by default - there was no-one else in the agency to do it. Through these early stumbling learning years from the late 1970's to the mid 1980's, I benefited enormously from the transparency created by the use of one-way screens. The people whom I was required by the institution to supervise also viewed my clinical work, so the transparency extended to me.

Over this time, I consistently noticed a distinction between my conversations and therapists' descriptions of the interactions between individual family members (☐Note 1). This difference often exposed uncontextualised truths held by the therapists.

R.T. Hare-Mustin (1994) sounded an alarm that continues to be relevant to the super-vision and therapy that I do. She describes the therapy room as 'lined with mirrors', where the discourses held by therapists and family members shape the meanings made of their conversations. These discourses may limit or assist us. However it is only when we know in what we are immersed, that we have the opportunity to negotiate the power relation inherent in the taking-up of one explanation or narrative over another.

Using one-way screens created a climate in which direct viewing of clinical practice was considered everyday, and invaluable in providing the means with which to identify the presuppositions by which the therapists were being guided. However I developed concerns about subjecting people (clients) to one-way screens, and experimented with ways to replicate the advantages produced by using one-way screens, while removing the ethical discomfort. Over time these experiments became the practice of 'prismatic dialogue'.

the context that supports discovery

The restructuring of New Zealand's social service institutions that began in the mid to late 1980's had a significant effect on the style of super-vision that I was being required to engage with. Business metaphors began to dominate, and leadership was repackaged into generalities with an emphasis on fiscal management. Clinical leadership became increasingly removed from direct clinical practice and mentorship.

During this time I was employed by institutions as an outside consultant to provide external super-vision within limited time frames. This created a context in which therapists/counsellors used super-vision principally to support their work in difficult or 'stuck' clinical situations. There was limited time available either to view or listen to the actual clinical work. I refused to call this 'super-vision', preferring to call it 'consultation' (Note 2).

The consultation process often felt like a pressure-cooker environment in which therapists presented the issues that they felt stuck with or desperate about. In turn, I felt pressured by the institutionally imposed time constraints to attempt to reduce the distress experienced by therapists. I noticed this pressure, and decided that I needed to change the way in which we were using the consultation process.

Initially, I withdrew from all super-vision and consultation relationships in order to focus on developing an intensive consultation/teaching environment. In this environment, participants met for one day, six times a year, with either David Epston or myself, and six times as a peer group. This context gave me the opportunity to experiment with different super-vision practices. After three years, I reconfigured the super-vision relational environment that I facilitated.

Throughout this period, I continued to be challenged by the desire to orientate my counselling and super-vision practice towards a collaborative enterprise, at the same time recognising the power relation inherent in this enterprise (☐Note 3). I was particularly interested in creating a super-vision environment in which the process of discovery was emphasised. This is in direct opposition to a super-vision style where one person (the facilitator) claims to hold objective knowledge about clinical concerns. Instead, I preferred to develop an experience in super-vision in which we did the following

- acknowledged the theoretical and experiential knowledge that we held
- used this knowledge to develop questions with an emphasis on relational language making (☐Note 4)
- readied ourselves to hear and experience the answer to these questions
- used this experience to develop another question and enquiry path
- reflected on the meaning made of our participation in the therapeutic and super-vision relationship

The experiential knowledge to which I am referring, includes the therapist's direct life experience, together with the imagined experience of the people (clients) with whom he/she is working. We are all susceptible to remaining immersed within our version of what is 'real' or 'true'.

However this position can have catastrophic effects on people's well-being when it is employed in counselling and in super-vision (Shotter, 1990). After three years of facilitating year-long consultation/training groups, I began to experiment with a conversational style that provided an experience of extra-vision in super-vision/consultation relationships.

David Epston and I decided to call the process that we were using in teaching contexts 'prismatic dialogue'. When I used prismatic dialogue in the context of super-vision, I would ask the therapist to imaginatively take up the position of the person with whom they were working. I would then interview the therapist, who answered the questions as though they were this person. This interview would last anywhere between five and thirty minutes.

I wanted therapists to experience a sense of 'extra-vision' as we moved to a place in which we could watch the subjective experience, utilise objective knowledge, and then develop a tentative relational enquiry, while we continued to watch the subjective experience. This conversational style created a spiral-like discovery process in which we were narrating or story-making in the present moment.

I found that prismatic dialogue enabled the therapist to experience movement. The movement was generated as we noticed the difference between the imagined subjectivity of the other (client), the subjective self, and the effect of this knowledge on the construction of the relationship and/or known theoretical ideas.

relational language-making and prismatic dialogue

I believe that the use of relational languaging is central to the creation of movement, and thus new narrative possibilities. Relational languaging encourages the interviewer to privilege the actual words used by others and our-selves, while protecting the relationship from the effects of totalisation and certainty. In other words, through using relational languaging, I can negotiate and expose the contextual and relational meaning of experiences such as the following:

diagram 1: conventional and relational language making

conventional language making	relational language making
I'm frustrated with you.	The frustration I experience when ...
I'm always pretending.	This pressure to pretend.
Do you think I'm over-involved?	Let's look at the type of involvement that works for therapeutic relationships.

When we use prismatic dialogue and relational language-making, the participants in super-vision identify direct experience, including imagining the direct experience of others (clients), in order to construct a relational perspective that offers new possibilities for exploration in the therapy.

As we move between direct experience and reflecting on this experience, we discover that our thoughts, feelings and actions are relationally and contextually shaped. I call this movement 'taking up the inside/outside position'. I believe that by generating this inside/outside reflexive process, we protect the super-vision/consultation relationship and the therapy/counselling relationship from meaning being imposed through the power relation.

I have drawn a line to link the two categories inside and outside. The movement between inside-direct-experience and outside-reflections-on-this-experience, creates a perspective that encourages the participants in super-vision to 'sense' the relational and contextual environment. This 'sense' represents the opening up of enough space to experience the implications of continuing to hold certain presuppositions, while bringing other possibilities to awareness.

I am emphasising the concept of 'bringing forward possibilities' in order to position us (facilitator/therapist/client) within a discovery process (☐Note 5). The inside/outside experience allows us to consider the contribution that therapists make to therapeutic relationships. Relationally re-searching this contribution encourages the development of a practical knowledge about the type of therapeutic relationship that people (clients) find both effective and representative of ethical professional boundaries.

I have experienced many challenges while facilitating super-vision relationships. The situations that I have found most taxing involved my use of the power relation to address ethical concerns. In these instances, relational consciousness and relational language-making supported me to navigate a process that could have easily floundered in a mire of defensiveness, accusation, shame, anger and subsequent detachment.

Through the years I have at times struggled to construct environments that promoted extension and challenge, while at the same time affirming competence. I now feel easier about the ability that I have to maintain this balance. However this ease is built on a number of agonisingly difficult situations. I hope that the ideas outlined here will help others to circumvent, or at least prepare for these challenges.

Throughout this book, I have primarily focused on describing the ideas and practices that I use in super-vision. I have emphasised the activity of super-vision, and accordingly I have highlighted the use of prismatic dialogue. I believe this process assists therapists to explore and find new inspiration possibilities, while attending to the power relation. Other relevant super-vision topics, such as super-vision contracts, are beyond the scope of this book.

CHAPTER 1

introducing
prismatic dialogue

Last week I began a teaching session by asking people to raise and lower their right arms. Then I asked them to repeat this; raising their right arms, while slowly breathing into their rib cages, using their back muscles to lift a relaxed arm and hand. People discovered a significant experiential difference in the two activities, although both could be described in the same way, 'I lifted my arm!'

Through this activity, I hoped people would re-consider the difference between the one-sided textual or spoken descriptions of therapeutic conversations, and the actual experiential process of negotiating meaning within a therapeutic conversation. When this difference is emphasised, our attention is inevitably drawn toward the construction of super-vision practices that prioritise experiential processes.

One of the principal experiential methods that I have developed for use in super-vision is 'prismatic dialogue'. This is a process in which a theory, belief, assumption, hypothesise or statement that we hold about others or ourselves (light) is passed through a number of imagined relational positions (prism). This process transforms the theory, belief, assumption, hypothesise or statement as we discover new experiential knowledges or possibilities (rainbow).

The use of prismatic dialogue assists counsellors to move from an observer position to relational subjectivity. Through relational subjectivity, we can experientially encounter the saying, 'The truth is in the eye of the beholder.' Once the processes for making and maintaining truths are exposed, then we can consider the effect on people of taking up one of the multiple ways that 'sense' can be made of life experiences.

Inevitably the above description excludes the living breathing interplay that occurs when we use words to bridge the physical space between us. We rarely articulate the way in which voice tone, tension, the partially said, the unsaid, the look, the smile, the physical presence and all that reverberates in the room, contributes to the meaning that we make of our participation in a conversation.

For many years, I experimented with ways to create experiential learning environments in which I was not reliant on the use of video-tapes or a one-way screen. Prismatic dialogue evolved through this experimentation.

Since 1988 I had employed the strategy of either asking participants in teaching environments to respond to the questions I asked from the imagined position of the person they were working with, or I asked them to take up both sides of a relationship dyad that they were a part of, such as mother/daughter, mother/son, father/daughter, father/son (Note 6). This practice developed as a consequence of my ongoing concerns about obtaining permission for the use of video or audio tape material (Note 7). This was particularly significant given the focus of my clinical work between 1988 to 1998 was with people who had suffered sexual, physical and emotional abuse.

In 1997, David Epston and I coined the term 'prismatic dialogue' to describe the principal teaching method we were using in year-long courses. The more I used prismatic dialogue in teaching and super-vision, the more apparent its benefits become. I discovered that prismatic dialogue sustained an attitude of discovery beyond the therapy room and into the super-vision process. Consequently, the therapeutic process was protected from a style of super-vision/consultation that confirmed the psychological theories held by either of the participants in the super-vision relationship.

I noticed that prismatic dialogue shifted people from stating and holding set positions, to experiencing the effect of inhabiting or taking up a position. Counsellors moved from searching for 'the right question' to noticing the effect of receiving the question from the position of the client. When I used people's (clients') actual expressions as the beginning point of a prismatic dialogue, we by-passed the therapist's conclusions and assumptions as we began the process of narrating (Bird, 2004. pp 139-146).

In prismatic dialogue, people's expressions are shifted into the relational in order to develop a consensual, contextual, meaning-making process (Bird, 2004). I have found this is particularly pertinent in super-vision/consultation, because counsellors are vulnerable to

- shifting experiential language into detached professional language
- creating a summary, or expressing the conclusion they have come to, as though this is true
- reconstituting people's (clients') actual language into expressions which are more familiar to counsellors/therapists
- using language conventionally, thereby generating absolutes and certainties around a significant meaning-making theme

Prismatic dialogue requires the participants in super-vision to engage in an interview in which the interview itself provides the material for discussion. This interview is only relevant if it is sustained or supported by the therapeutic relationship which has already been developed between the therapist and the person (client). This directly contrasts a super-vision process in which one person (consultant/facilitator) gives another person (counsellor/therapist) advice, presents detached questions, or tells the counsellor/therapist what is 'really' happening.

A number of therapy traditions have utilised the strategy of interviewing a person who is imaginatively representing someone else's responses and reactions (Roth and Chasin, 1994; Epston, 1993). I have departed from these traditions by using relational languaging to construct a prismatic dialogue in which experience can be relationally and contextually viewed or engaged with. Such a prismatic dialogue includes

- conducting a thirty to forty minute long prismatic interview that is audio-taped, and this audio-tape is taken back to people (clients) for comment and reflection
- a five to ten minute long prismatic interview in which the counsellor experiences the development of a different conversational direction

Prismatic dialogue allows me to expose the effect of power relations on the making sense process, rather than being subject to the power relation through 'truth' assumptions.

Counsellors experience a sense of movement as they engage in prismatic dialogue. Invariably this movement produces awareness of new possibilities for therapeutic directions and conversations. I believe one of the principal tasks of super-vision is to liberate the mind in order to foster the counsellor's sense of creativity.

stepping through
the prismatic dialogue process

This is the process I use when engaging with a prismatic dialogue:

- At the beginning of the process, the counsellor 'introduces' the person (client) to the participants, while imagining that the person (client) is present in the room. This instruction helps the counsellor avoid theorising or using psychological or detached descriptions of people's experience. I shape the introduction in this way, 'People sometimes use this process when they think the therapy needs new ideas or directions. What do I need to know to understand where the therapy is up to?'

- The counsellor physically moves position into another chair. She/he then attempts to represent the subjective experience of the person (client). I begin the interview by using the person's (client's) name to address the counsellor.

- In a recent consultation, for example, a counsellor represented the difficulties that she was having in reducing Lilly's (client's) anxiety. The counsellor described Lilly as 'anxious intermittently'. When I asked the counsellor to represent Lilly, we (consultant and counsellor) discovered within the first three questions that the language Lilly used to describe the experience she had was this, 'Fundamentally, I'm worried that when I go to University, I'll lose my boyfriend and my friends.'

  The counsellor had previously concluded that Lilly was suffering from high levels of anxiety and had acted on this theory by suggesting ideas for reducing 'her anxiety'. The specific contextual environment within which Lilly was immersed was consequently unavailable to the therapy and to Lilly.

  The worry that we identified was specific, 'the worry that I will lose my boyfriend and friends'. When this particular worry was explored contextually, we discovered Lilly was the first person in her extended family to attend University. It was also a rarity in her neighbourhood for young people to attend University.

Consequently, this worry was located within a cultural, family and socio-economic context.

- The prismatic dialogue concludes once the therapist discovers new possibilities for exploration or conversation. This can take between five and fifty minutes.

- The entire prismatic consultation interview can be audio-taped. The audio-tape can be used in these ways:

  - As a reflective tool for the therapy, when people (counsellor and client) listen to the audio tape together. The listening process is once again negotiated. Sometimes people (clients) choose to listen to the interviewer's question, stop the tape and then respond to the question. The tape is then turned on and both people listen to the counsellor's response.

    People (clients) may also prefer to listen to the entire tape before reflecting on the interview. Throughout the interview, there is an opportunity to comment on the differences and similarities between the counsellor and clients' responses.

    It is important that the counsellor orientates her/himself toward discovery, rather than being 'right' or 'correct'. If there is a difference between the counsellor's response and the person's (client's) response, this difference can be re-searched within the bounds of the therapeutic relationship understanding. In other words, any re-search needs to be of benefit to the therapy.

  - Alternatively, questions can be extracted from the audio-tape of the interview and taken back to the person (client) for comment.

escaping binary oppositions

In some situations the therapy can seem to be trapped between two positions, with the person (client) either oscillating between the two positions or taking up a single definitive position. This definitive position can be taken up even though it has negative effects on the person's life, because the other position seems so untenable. In this context, the counsellor often holds back from stating a position, even though she/he continues to have definite views about which position is preferable.

In this example, I am using a prismatic dialogue in the interview with Lee (counsellor) who takes up the position of Claire (client). Lee describes a situation in which she feels she is struggling to help Claire challenge the fear that she is HIV positive. Claire has refused to have a test to review her HIV status and is terrified for her life.

Claire (Lee)	I can't ... you ... I've had unprotected sex. I probably have got HIV ... That means. You know. I looked forward to my life having children, giving my mum grandchildren.
Johnella	So this fear that you might have HIV, how much is it permeating everything at the moment?
Claire (Lee)	Everything. I just can't stop thinking about it.
Johnella	OK. So this fear is permeating the present. It's permeating now, the present moment, but it's also being taken into the future with you thinking, 'If this fear is true then certain things will happen.'
Claire (Lee)	Yes. I'm so pissed with myself because I know it was dangerous. Why did I give in to his pressure?

I made a decision to put to one side 'the pressure he applied to her', in order to focus on the terror Claire was experiencing. This issue can be investigated later through a possible link to 'the paralysing effect of fear', that is, the fear of rejection or the fear of anger, and so on.

Johnella	In the present moment in your listening to this fear, is there any joy? Any pleasure in your life?
Claire (Lee)	No.
Johnella	This fear's taking every drop of energy, pleasure and joy in this moment?
Claire (Lee)	Yeah. That's it.
Johnella	OK. So in living with this fear which is taking every drop of energy, pleasure, joy from you. Is this fear like living with the diagnosis?
Claire (Lee)	Yes, it is.
Johnella	If you had the diagnosis would anything be different? Would you discover anything different than you're discovering right now?
Claire (Lee)	Well, that would be it then.
Johnella	Is there any bit of you that says in a determined way, 'It isn't this. I haven't got HIV.'
Claire (Lee)	No.

Johnella	So you're living as though this is true? You're living in the truth of this even though you don't know this?
Claire (Lee)	Well. It's ... It's ...
Johnella	OK. What's different from living in the truth of this even though you don't know this and having a test which tells you it's true or it's not? What would be different?
Claire (Lee)	... I suppose if I did the test and I did know, that would really be it. It wouldn't be worth going on.
Johnella	What's the difference between every minute of your life now, all the joy, all the pleasure being soaked up by this fear and what would be different?
Claire (Lee)	I don't know the answer to this. I think Claire would say, 'I might decide to kill myself.'
Johnella	OK. Then you might decide to kill yourself. That would be the difference. Let me summarise a little bit. There's living in a jail of misery that you're living in now not knowing - living as though the diagnosis is true - but not knowing. Then we have knowing and living in a jail of misery and deciding to kill yourself. And then we have the possibility of finding out 'I don't have HIV,' ... Which one do you feel drawn toward?
Claire (Lee)	Finding out I don't have HIV.
Johnella	That one is only possible through a test. You have these other two, without the test. But this one will come only with the test.
Claire (Lee)	Yes, that's true.
Johnella	OK. Take up your place Lee, I want to speak to you.
	Lee, I might go on to say to Claire, 'How would life change if you thought, 'I don't have HIV'? If you had this test would there be any more joy in life? It seems the test is the only thing that has any hope with it. The other options only carry despair.'
	Lee, you will notice there is a persistent quality to this interview style. I need to understand and expose the fears Claire has, in order to find a way that Claire can either survive these fears or act on these fears.

Through this prismatic dialogue, Lee directly experienced the effect of exploring and presenting the dilemma that Claire was struggling with. Consequently, Lee identified that the therapy had become stuck as she gently advocated for or persuaded Claire to take the test.

Lee acknowledged that this had occurred before she had sufficiently explored and exposed the dilemma that Claire was facing.

preparing to listen to the tape

When the therapy seems to be stuck in some way, I will often suggest that we audio-tape a prismatic dialogue. This is often very useful when the counsellor identifies that she/he is pushing against a strongly held presupposition. Lynetta (counsellor) for example, found herself struggling to counter Jai's argument. Jai had embarked on a journey of seeking justice through the court system for the rape she suffered. Although she felt vindicated by a guilty verdict she was incensed by the sentence. In counselling, she said

Jai There is no justice. Justice was promised to me and I was betrayed. I can't survive without justice. I'll have to take my own justice.

Lynetta wanted to protect Jai from experiencing another 'professional' arguing against her position. However she was also concerned about the type of action Jai might take in order to find 'Justice'. She found herself doing very little with Jai's comments apart from affirming her distress. In this instance, Lynetta and I engaged in a recorded prismatic dialogue in which Lynetta represented Jai. This audio-tape was taken back to the counselling and supported Jai and Lynetta to discuss both the concept of 'Justice' and the 'type of Justice' that Jai could pursue that would also enhance her life.

The way in which people (clients) listen to the tape is a negotiation between counsellor and client. As I mentioned earlier, people have found it useful to

- listen to the facilitator's/consultant's taped question
- turn the tape off. The person answers the question
- turn the tape on and listen to the counsellor/therapist's answer
- discuss similarities and differences
- organise a signal for requesting that the tape be turned off
- negotiate who turns the tape on and off. Ideally both people can be involved in this

I suggest that counsellor and client initially listen jointly to the tape for these reasons:

- Differences and errors of representation can be discussed immediately.

- This prevents any meaning being made and held by the person (client) which may interfere with the collaborative intention of the therapy.

- The experience of listening to a conversation in which one person attempts to represent the direct life experiences of another can be unpredictable.

    Inevitably, counsellors will be using their imaginative ability to guess responses to questions that haven't yet been asked in the therapy. When these guesses are accurate this can be experienced as overwhelming. This is particularly relevant for people who have survived traumatic experiences by using strategies of 'invisibility' or 'disappearing' themselves.

    This possibility can be raised prior to listening to the tape in order to negotiate safety strategies (Bird, 2000. pp 205-206). One essential safety strategy, for example, is to encourage people (clients) to listen for and notice any changes in the body and/ or emotional affect. It is important to then negotiate ways of signalling this as part of the reflective process.

- In order to use the prismatic dialogue effectively, the emotional, physical and intellectual responses that occur while listening to the tape are taken notice of. Once these responses are identified, we re-search what this means.

- When differences are identified between the counsellor's imaginatively informed response and the person's direct experience, these differences are regarded as discoveries. This challenges the notion that the counsellor has got it wrong. These differences provide resources for exploration which may have remained unavailable to the therapy without the prismatic dialogue.

After the first listening session, the use of the tape can be negotiated. Some people want to listen to it again at home, while others want the tape kept within the therapeutic context.

group super-vision and prismatic dialogue

When the prismatic dialogue occurs within group super-vision, one person can be nominated as a scribe who records the questions. This process is useful when the prismatic dialogue is used to move the therapy from a stuck place by producing a number of new exploration possibilities.

Team members can act as a reflecting team to the therapy (⬚Note 8). This reflection can also be audio-taped or transcribed and taken back to the therapy.

Sometimes the prismatic dialogue or prismatic consultation is audio taped and transcribed by the counsellor with copies circulated to members of the group and the person (client) for study and review purposes.

post-interview follow-up

After people have listened to the tape, they (counsellor/client) can reflect on the experience by answering questions such as:

➡ What was your response to listening to the interview?

➡ What stood out for you in the interview?

➡ Would you like to add or change anything?

➡ How could I have represented the experiences you have shared with me differently?

➡ Are there any questions you would have liked the interviewer to have asked?

➡ While being interviewed, trying to stand in your shoes, I found myself feeling/thinking/considering ... Is this similar or different for you?

➡ What would you like the team to know or hear about you or from you?

The next two examples reflect different uses of the prismatic dialogue process. The first represents a joint post-interview conversation which is part of the ongoing therapy, whereas the second represents people's (counsellor and clients) individual responses to listening to the prismatic dialogue.

 prismatic dialogue

The following conversation took place between Libby (client) and Raewyn (counsellor), after they listened to an audio-tape in which Raewyn was interviewed as Libby, using the prismatic dialogue process.

Libby	It was really good hearing someone else's point of view in my shoes. Knowing what they felt and that they were understanding what I was going through. I was surprised that someone understood what I meant.
Raewyn	What was that like, knowing that someone understands what it's like?
Libby	About bloody time! (laughter)
Raewyn	How does it help to know that someone has some vague idea of what it's like in your shoes?
Libby	It makes it easy to talk to them. I have a lot of trouble saying things. If they don't get it right the first or second times I get angry because I can't express it so that they understand. And it is really hard, and frustration goes inside and becomes anger.

- - -

Raewyn	What do you think about the conversation we had on the tape?
Libby	It was quite good listening to it. I did laugh sometimes because you did get a few things wrong to do with anger, but we are not all perfect. I'm twenty-five not twenty-three, and I have had lots of Parenting courses, but I never had a chance to use what I had.
Raewyn	You had the theory, but you never put it into practice before?
Libby	No.

- - -

Libby	Johnella had really good questions. I was able to answer them myself before you came on. I could answer them myself.
Raewyn	What were some of the good questions?
Libby	The anger ones.
Raewyn	Any particular ... around the anger ones?
Libby	To do with my daughter's crying... like the first thing is admitting you have a problem, second thing is looking for something to do about it, the third thing is going for it, doing something about it. It is like a stepping stone. Like an AA course.
Raewyn	So did somehow these questions provide stepping stones for you?
Libby	Yes. Like in class we are learning to keep our kids safe, keep ourselves safe. To close our eyes and pretend we are in another place to calm ourselves down. I've tried it a few times and it did work. It was something I could

	do before I went in to deal with my crying daughter. It's putting a kit together. A resource to use. Listening to the tape and the time between then and now, I have started to build up a resource kit.
Raewyn	Were there any questions that really stuck out for you as useful questions?
Libby	'What has been supporting your parenting?' It made me think. It made me look at the two, what was negative and what was positive, what was good for me and what wasn't, what was working and what to look for next time. And the question, 'When the pressure to 'get it right' is around, where is the anger? Is anger around as well or not around?' Yes. It is. Because this is my third chance to get it right. I have to find what suits me, what the support is like, how they use confidentiality. If things happen, what do they do about it? It is a lot of questioning. I needed to know that you can work things through before they go to C.Y.F.S. So I had to go through a lot of questioning before I found the right place (☐Note 9).

- - -

Raewyn	Was there anything else that you wanted the team to hear about?
Libby	For me it's been really hard. I've got three kids but two of them were taken off me. It's not very easy being a mother by yourself. You're a two in one. A mother and father in one. It's really hard.
Raewyn	When Johnella was asking questions about the effects of scrutiny, how spot on were they for you?
Libby	They were really good. It's like being under a spotlight ... no, not a spotlight, a magnifying glass.
Raewyn	Where every small imperfection gets enlarged?
Libby	Yes. It's very hard. Especially if it is C.Y.F.S. You have to do everything absolutely perfect!
Raewyn	So you have to get it more right than every other mother did?
Libby	Yes. You have to be right. If you slap the kid, C.Y.F.S. is in, 'You are not meant to be doing that, I'm sorry but we are taking the kid.'
Raewyn	All the things that you were told about, you could see other mothers doing just as badly, and no one taking any notice, but you were the one with finger pointed at you. You were the one whose child was taken off you, not once but twice. And you were the one with the third child, struggling really

hard, wanting to keep that child, but being aware that you were under the magnifying glass.

Libby   Yes. Yes (▢Note 10).

- - -

For the reader's information: Libby was not sent into this programme by The Child, Youth and Family Service. It was her choice to ensure that things would be different with this child.

prismatic dialogue

In this instance Sara (client) was discussing with Erena (counsellor) the struggle she was having to find a way to live after the tragic death of her son Tim. Erena hoped that the prismatic dialogue would provide her and Sara with ideas to discuss. I also hoped to use the video-tape in teaching environments, to demonstrate the unique nature of a discovery process that prioritises each person's ways of making sense of life experiences.

After Sara and Erena reviewed a video-tape of the prismatic dialogue between Erena and Johnella, they made these comments:

Sara's (client's) response to the prismatic dialogue

It was very close to me, to what I'd say - some different tones - but really close to what I'd say. It must have been a hard interview (for both Erena and Johnella) but that is what I'm like. I move around emotionally a lot. Ideas and questions bring more questions, which is good but hard too.

Seeing Tim's photo, knowing Johnella has 'met' him too now ... and going to South Africa, England and Norway with her. Well, he's travelling too you see ... and he always wanted to travel and well, now he is. He's going to all those people who will know him a little bit too ... This way he is growing, not staying static ... and I have started to give away his things like his leather jacket (the guitar I'm not quite ready for!) Alex didn't take the jacket off all night ... He left saying, 'I'll wear it to band practice,' and in this way I realised Tim would be there (at band practice with his mates) too and that he is growing with them ...

I will have to think more about that question of what I listen for, what I notice ... Tim and I had a great belief in readiness, in the right time for things ... I don't know how I work out the timing but I will think more about that question ... Overall, I felt very understood.

Erena's (counsellor's) response to the post-prismatic dialogue

It's been quite a powerful experience for me because the work with Sara is quite strong, and the depth of thinking she brings to our conversations can't be met with glib answers.

Experiencing the significance of the space for the ongoing deep despair and pain Sara feels, has been important to me. It allows me to not push in those moments, because this place of pain seems to be the only place from which any glimmer of hope seems possible and visible (to Sara). This is quite different from the simplistic counselling notions of over-emphasising hope or models which push for the pain, with the view of 'emptying the grief' with the belief that then moving on is possible.

Realising I need to slow down and ask more linking detailed questions like, 'What tells you? What do you first notice?'

common dilemmas

Prismatic dialogue can raise these issues for the counsellor being interviewed:

- I can't answer this question because I have never experienced a situation like this.

  In this instance the counsellor is entering unknown territory as he/she has come up to the edge of the direct experiential knowledge that she/he holds.

- I can't answer this question because I don't know exactly how the person (client) would answer this.

  In the prismatic dialogue the counsellor is required to access the experiential knowledge she/he hold about the other (client). Sometimes the prismatic interview reveals that the counsellor/therapist has been primarily privileging psychological generalisations about the person's life. In other instances, the question goes beyond the therapist's/counsellor's imaginings of the experiential life of the other person (client).

  Whenever the counsellor who is taking up the imagined position of the person (client) finds her/himself at her/his imaginative limit, I will speak directly to the intention which informed the question. In speaking to the intention that supports the question, I hope to encourage dialogue between counsellor and client and provide support for the counsellor's imaginative ability. I believe this intention must be languaged relationally in order to use this as a tentative meaning platform. When intention is constructed to support a tentative meaning platform, there is room for exploration and change (Bird, 2004. pp 174-175).

👫 prismatic dialogue

In this prismatic dialogue, Marg is representing Zoe (her client). Zoe is contemplating making changes to her husband's study. He died one year ago. Marg who represents Zoe couldn't answer a question I asked because Marg had not explored this with Zoe. I responded in this way:

Johnella   OK. I'll talk a little about the thinking behind this question. I'm attempting to ask a question that allows you to imagine the effects on you of making changes to the study. I am hoping that if we can predict these effects, you might be able to put protective strategies in place as you decide what will stay and what will go.

Zoe (Marg)   I don't think anything will protect me. No. That's not entirely true. It really helped to have my sister there when I needed to sell the car.

When I (interviewer) expose the intention that shapes a question this provides the therapist and client with a possibility or an idea on which to reflect.

- I can't answer this question because I don't want to imagine this possibility.

Prismatic dialogue encourages the counsellor to subjectively respond to questions. Through this subjective response, the counsellor feels the impact of the question and the answer.

The imagination can be used as a resource to transport counsellors into territory beyond their direct experience. When counsellors enter this space they can find themselves entertaining life possibilities which they have previously avoided, such as the death of a child, a life-threatening illness, the murder of a parent, sexual abuse perpetrated by a family friend.

Within this space, counsellors can experience strong emotions (such as fear, anxiety, revulsion, love or anger). Once these strong emotions are noticed and named, they become a site for exploration. This exploration is used to re-search the effects of these emotions on the therapist and on the therapeutic process.

I believe an essential element of collaborative conversations is the counsellor's ability to imaginatively entertain the dilemmas the person (client) is experiencing. At times, counsellors have identified a restraint to imaginatively considering a life possibility or dilemma such as 'I'm afraid to imagine the possibility that I could suddenly fall ill and die.' Once this is identified, we can explore the nature of this restraint.

The imaginative process that I am suggesting involves the ability to consider a life-possibility, while also witnessing or considering the effect of living with this life dilemma. When experience is relationally languaged, the person is neither detached from the experience, nor immersed in the experience.

Relational language-making allows people to come back to a place between inside-direct-experience and outside-reflecting-on-direct-experience. The interviewer is sensitive to this movement and attempts to hold the inside/outside boundary line by relationally attending to feelings and experiences.

Interviewer   As you remember the loss of ... , is the sadness moving you back into the past memories or are you aware of yourself, here in the room, looking back to the past?

■   The questions move me into representing the experiences that I have or had in my life. In this place I struggle to represent the other person because I am propelled into my direct experience.

In this instance, all participants in the conversation work together to ascertain the effect on the therapy of the counsellor's direct life experiences. We attempt to find ways to support the counsellor to maintain relational consciousness or an outsider/insider position within the therapy. If it becomes apparent that the counsellor is ongoingly struggling to maintain this position, then we negotiate a process for ethically ending the therapy while referring the person (client) to another counsellor.

The above issues can all limit the counsellor's ability to engage with relational consciousness and take up the contributor position within the therapeutic relationship (Bird, 2004. pp 181-195). It is the task of super-vision/consultation to identify these issues and support the counsellor to either reposition her/himself within the therapeutic relationship or extend the experiential knowledges that she/he has. It is the function of super-vision/consultation to address the issues raised in the previous examples.

In most instances, the super-vision/consultation process provides an environment in which counsellors' experiential knowledges are considered and extended, in order to meet the challenges presented in the therapeutic relationship. In rare instances, the vulnerabilities evoked by the interview may reveal to the counsellor that she/he is unable to manage the inside/outside position. In these circumstances, the counsellor can be assisted in negotiating the end of a particular therapeutic relationship.

prismatic dialogue and time

The prismatic dialogue can last anywhere between five minutes to an hour. I may use a five minute conversation to demonstrate negotiating a stuck point in the therapy. In a thirty minute or hour long dialogue, I might experiment with developing a new contextual understanding for the therapy. Through this process, I hope that counsellors experience new possibilities, that in turn engender the type of freshness that inspires creativity. Prismatic dialogue acts to reconnect counsellors with creative possibilities, rather than the provision of definitive answers.

As counsellors are describing a situation, I may ask them to take up the position of the person they're describing and conduct a five minute interview with them. I begin a prismatic dialogue, in order to experiment with a new conversational direction. Counsellors who are involved as participants will often notice

- they have assumed an understanding rather than negotiated this understanding. In other words, counsellors have leapt ahead of people (clients)
- a difference in the life values held by the counsellor and the people they work with
- a strong emotion held by either participant (counsellor and client). This unnegotiated emotional response remains influential in respect to meaning-making
- the effect of a taken-for-granted psychological truth
- a dedication to a particular outcome rather than negotiating the outcome with people (clients)

- a backgrounding and sometimes neglect of the effect on people of participating in a therapeutic relationship

The five minute prismatic dialogue is an effective way to demonstrate the skills required to develop new contextual understandings. Consequently super-vision becomes a site for extending the actual therapeutic practice of counsellors. At the completion of the prismatic dialogue, these questions are available to be reflected on by the counsellor:

➡ What did you discover that had previously been unknown or unavailable to you?

➡ Which ideas/practices/circumstances supported that unavailability?

➡ How will you use this discovery as a wondering or a possibility in the therapy?

➡ Will this discovery impact on the clinical practice you use beyond this specific interview?

the benefits of prismatic dialogue

This way of conducting super-vision/consultation/training seems to be effective for these reasons:

- It creates an environment that illuminates the often complex, contradictory and fragmentary nature of direct experience. The use of relational language-making allows us to prioritise, explore and extend the everyday language people use to represent their experience. Prioritising people's expressions protects them from being subjected to any counsellor's assumption of meaning. Consequently, the emphasis is on negotiating meaning rather than searching for 'truth' or answers.

- Unlike most super-vision/consultation/training processes, the prismatic dialogue can be made fully available to the therapy. People (clients) can comment on any assumptions and theories exposed in the prismatic dialogue because we are prioritising everyday language to express experiences.

- Listening to one person's (counsellor's) attempts to empathise deeply with another's (clients) experience can have profound effects. It can be a moment in which a person (client) can feel comprehensively understood or seen by another. It can provide an experience of the therapy that affirms to the person that she/he is a 'unique participant' in the conversation, rather than a person that is scrutinised and objectified by another.

- The activity of listening to an audio-tape and/or reading a transcript creates an opportunity for the person (client) to become an audience to the representation (by the counsellor) of her/his experiences. From the audience position, the person can reflect on ideas and feelings rather than being swamped or immersed in the conversation. The inside/outside experience that is generated by prismatic dialogue, allows for new envisaging or experiences of the self in relationship to the identified concerns, significant others and the therapeutic relationship. Roth and Chasin write about using psychodramatic techniques to achieve a similar effect (1994. pp 204).

- The counsellor is supported in imaginatively engaging with life dilemmas. Through the use of relational language-making, the counsellor relates to the significant everyday metaphoric representations of experience (⬚Note 11). This positioning situates the person as inside/outside of direct experience. The insider/outsider (relational consciousness) position allows people to experience a question, a dilemma, a response while at the same time, remaining a witness or audience to this question, dilemma or response. The counsellor is held away from entering personal, direct experience by the interviewer's sensitivity to

  - use of relational language-making

  - changes of affect, including the appearance of a strong emotional response

  - body responses, including signs of detachment from the process

  - the flow of the interview. Do the presented themes flow from the conversation or is the counsellor directing the conversation in some way?

Prismatic dialogue supports transparency in therapy and super-vision/consultation as it moves the therapy out from behind closed doors to be viewed by colleagues and clients. In this climate of transparency, the search for understanding becomes apparent to all participants. The collaborative intention of the therapy is represented in action. The mystique of the professional classes represented as those who know us better than ourselves, dissolves with the knowledge that all participants in the conversation (client, counsellor, consultant) are searching for understanding in the collaborative process of conversation or dialogue.

The counsellor has a direct experience of the conversation from the person's (client's) position. This can promote a significant understanding and knowledge of the experiential lives of people (clients) as counsellors get a glimpse of the emotional consequences of a question or a direction of enquiry. This can assist the counsellor to appreciate rather than take-for-granted what can initially appear as commonplace (☐Note 12).

Engaging in a conversation that illuminates the complexity of people's (clients') lives, requires the counsellor to reconsider her/his understandings, experiences and relationship to these complexities. This process can highlight areas of concern that may be limiting the counsellor's engagement with the person (client).

extra-vision through prismatic dialogue

I commented earlier that I use prismatic dialogue in a variety of ways over different time frames, from a five minute consultation process through to an hour-long consultation with a reflecting team. I have found prismatic dialogue supports super-vision in these ways

- exposing the binary positions that entrap people (clients) and limit the therapy

- once the binary positions are exposed we can experiment with finding new positions to inhabit

- negotiating and exploring the contradictory and fragmentary nature of gender, class, cultural, sexuality relations rather than taking up positions (including no position)

- coming up to the edge of the counsellor's experiential life and extending this knowledge through the clinical work

- extending the counsellor's imaginative resource

- working with a stuck place in the therapy

- emphasising the process of discovery rather static knowledge

- extending the counsellor's technical abilities

- practising processes for negotiating ethical positions with people (clients), for example, therapeutic relationship boundaries

- exposing the taken-for-granted truths the counsellor holds

- moving the theoretical constructs held by the counsellor into a living practice

In the following section, I have included several examples of the different ways in which I have used prismatic dialogue. I have also presented an entire transcript of an interview to illustrate the ebb and flow of therapeutic conversations. It is often useful to read these conversations out loud (□Note 13).

Counsellors who are attracted to collaborative approaches can find themselves feeling 'stuck' in therapeutic conversations when confronted by the definitive beliefs held by people (clients). These definitive beliefs can be held about the self, 'I'm worthless/stupid/ugly/ignorant/bad/wrong' or held about others, 'She/he is ridiculous/stupid/over-emotional/irrational/wrong.'

♀♂ prismatic dialogue

In the next example, the counsellor is presenting a situation in which she found herself doing and saying nothing in regard to a comment made by Jack. She couldn't think of a way to usefully reflect on both the intention that shaped this comment and the possible effect of this comment on others. The stuck place represented here is commonly experienced when counsellors are confronted with people's (clients') strongly held beliefs about other people who occupy a cultural/gendered/sexuality/class/age/wellness position. For example, 'All poofters deserve to be beaten up.'

The primary purpose of this interview was to provide Sally with an experience of moving beyond feeling silenced. I hoped she would then be resourced to experiment with enquiry processes in similar situations.

Sally presented the dilemma that she had experienced:

In a drug and alcohol therapeutic group, Fred (a group participant) said something like, 'I've been in and out of this relationship that's been going on, but I'm finally out of it. She's an ex-stripper, and you know ... , but I don't want to go into that right now. But anyway there's this relationship.'

Then another participant Jack said, 'Shame, that would have been good, to hear stories about wet t-shirt competitions and jelly wrestling.' At this point, I had the dilemma of what to do with these comments. I decided to say nothing, but I felt I'd let an opportunity go by.

Subsequently I asked Sally to take the position of Jack for this prismatic dialogue.

Johnella	What would be a shame about the fact that Fred who has been attempting to leave this relationship for a long time has finally left it? You said that was a shame, what did you mean by that?
Jack	Oh ... Umm … What did I mean?
Johnella	What were you hoping Fred might take from that?
Jack	I don't know. I was kind of looking forward to hearing the stories and I just thought he's probably missing out on something with being with someone like that.
Johnella	So you were attempting to convince him to stay in this relationship?
Jack	Well, you know what these women are like.
Johnella	What are they like?
Jack	Well. When they have lifestyles like that, you know he'd be missing out on a whole lot of good stuff.
Johnella	Like what? What's the good stuff you're thinking about?
Jack	Do we have to talk about this here?
Johnella	I'm really curious about the good stuff that you think he might be missing out on.
Jack	I'm sure the other blokes understand what I'm saying.
Johnella	They might, but I'd really like to understand as well. What's the good things that you think Jack might be missing out on?
Jack	Well. You know women like that. She'd probably be pretty easy I think.
Johnella	Are you talking about the ease in the relationship or easy in which way?
Jack	Oh. This is a bit strange. I'm mean this is drug and alcohol (the setting) I don't know if I want to talk about this here.
Johnella	Actually, you know drug and alcohol, I don't know if you've noticed, but I have over the years, drug and alcohol is a bit about all sorts of things. Drug and alcohol is a lot about life, and so that's why I'm interested. What do you think would be good about this relationship, and what would be easy about this relationship?
Jack	Probably the sex I guess.
Johnella	The sex.
Jack	Mmm.

Johnella	So this idea that, when you're talking to Fred and saying, are you saying to him, 'How could you have left her? I mean the sex must have been great?' is that what you were saying?

The tone of my voice will affect the meaning made of the previous questions. If Jack had said, 'I'm not going to talk about it. You know what I mean,' I would have responded, 'I can have a read between the lines - guess about what was meant. However I'd be concerned that I might guess wrong and you'd experience this as judgemental.' If Jack reassured me that there would be no judgement in respect to this guess then I would present an interpretation. I would then re-search how close my guess was to his understanding.

Jack	Yeh. I guess that's part of it.
Johnella	Easy sex.
Jack	Sort of sex on tap I guess.
Johnella	Sex on tap. What is sex on tap?
Jack	Oh. Whenever you want it I guess.
Johnella	OK.
Jack	Obviously she'd have to go out working the hours she works.
Johnella	Sex on tap would be, you just turn on the tap and sex happens.
Jack	When you want it.
Johnella	When you want it.
Jack	Mmm.
Johnella	With a person like this do you think you'd have to negotiate sex, or ask for sex, or she'd have to want sex, or is it a two way wanting or is it a one way wanting?
Jack	I don't know, I guess she'd know how to treat a man right and how to umm ... , with some you've got to con them into it, or spend all this time talking about feeling stuff ... , that she'd just know what it's about.
Johnella	What is it about, from your point of view? What is the sexual knowledge you hope she'd carry that you think many other women don't because you'd have to use a con, you'd have to talk them into it? What do think the sexual knowledge is that she'd carry?
Jack	Maybe giving you sex when you wanted it.

Johnella	The sexual knowledge she would carry would be, 'Give him sex when he wants it.'
Jack	Mmm. I mean she's working in a field where she knows how to please men.
Johnella	She's working in a field where she gives men sex when they want it.
Jack	Mmm kind of, yeh.
Johnella	So in this field that she's working in, is there any exchange for sex? Does she get anything from it?
Jack	She gets paid for her job.
Johnella	OK. So there's money with it?
Jack	Mmm.
Johnella	Do you think Jack, did Fred do that? Did he pay her too? In their relationship, was that the exchange?
Jack	I don't know, you'd have to ask Fred.
Johnella	Would you?
Jack	Would I pay?
Johnella	Yeh. If, you know, you're in a relationship with this woman, would you sort of go, 'Well. OK. She's somebody who has a sexual knowledge that I like. She's somebody that will give me sex when I want it, and in exchange I give her, eighty dollars or the going rate'?
Jack	Not if I was going out with her. No.
Johnella	So there's a difference. What would be the exchange if you were going out with her?
Jack	Well. She'd get to hang with me.
Johnella	And what benefit would that be for her? What would she like about that? What would she enjoy about that? What would be good about that?
Jack	I'm pretty easy going and I'm not unreasonable. She wouldn't have to do much cleaning,
Johnella	OK. You're easy going. There'd be not much cleaning. Anything else she'd get out of this relationship with you?
Jack	Oh, a few laughs. I like to have a few laughs.
Johnella	Laughs. If you were sort of selling yourself to a person and you were going, 'Look. In this relationship I get to have sex whenever I want it, and you get someone who you can have a few laughs with, is easy going, and is ... , doesn't need too much cleaning,' do you think that person would be drawn to that description of a relationship?
Jack	You make it sound strange when you say it like that.

Johnella	What do you think? Fill me in. What's the missing link here? Like you think there's something strange in what I'm saying? What's missing in this description?
Jack	Well. She'd obviously want to be with me if she was with me. I'm kind of cute.
Johnella	Cute.
Jack	Mmm.
Johnella	OK. So there'd be some desire to be in the relationship because you're cute.
Jack	Mmm.
Johnella	Anything else that might draw someone to the relationship?
Jack	I've got quite a bit of world knowledge too I guess, of life experience.
Johnella	Life experience. Do you think that there'd be any possibility that the person you might get into a relationship with might want to also negotiate being sexual with you, when they want it?
Jack	It's just hard to talk about that stuff though. I can't imagine that sort of conversation.
Johnella	You're doing pretty well here.
Jack	Well, you won't let me not answer!
Johnella	That's right. OK. So it's a bit of a hard conversation. Do you think it would be hard for other people in the group to talk about how you talk to women and talk amongst yourselves about being sexual?
Jack	Mmm. I think it's pretty hard.
Johnella	Does this group - apart from when we're here - does this group talk about this, about how to negotiate being sexual?
Jack	No. they don't talk about that stuff in group.
Johnella	What do you think would support you guys to talk about this stuff?
Jack	I can't really think.
Johnella	OK. Jack, when you said that to Fred, you know about, 'It'd be great and you'd be getting all the sex you wanted,' are there any other things, other than that, that you'd want to know about the relationship he had with her?
Jack	It was just a kind of throwaway comment.
Johnella	Oh, a throwaway comment.
Jack	Mmm.

Johnella	So if you weren't throwing away this comment, if you were making a comment you wanted Fred to take seriously, what would you ask him?
Jack	I don't know, I wasn't really even thinking of saying anything serious to him. Do you think I'm disrespectful? I'm not meaning anything about the women in here. Like I really like women.
Johnella	Good. I suppose I was quite interested in how we know when a comment is a 'throwaway'. I'm assuming you mean not to take seriously.
Jack	Mmm.
Johnella	How will we know when something is a throwaway comment and how will we know when it's not? How would you know if a comment was throwaway and how would you know when it wasn't throwaway?
Jack	You kind of get a sense. Sometimes people laugh, I guess. I mean, Bob laughed when I said that.
Johnella	Yeah. Have you ever found that at times you've laughed about a throwaway comment, and then the comment is taken seriously? Have you ever found that?
Jack	Mmm. Yes. At the pub I guess that's happened.
Johnella	Is it hard, or have you found it hard, or have you found it easy, to make a comment about what's a laugh? I mean if you've taken something seriously is it easy or hard for you to say, 'Look that throwaway comment is not OK'?
Jack	I don't say that. I just finish my beer and go.
Johnella	OK. So sometimes other people's throwaway comments can be taken up seriously.
Jack	Mmm. Do you think that's happened here?
Johnella	I don't know. I suppose in a little way I've taken it seriously. You know it's like what does this comment mean? And in a way we've found out that it does mean quite a lot actually. You know it means there's some ideas about sex, ideas about what you appreciate in a relationship and what you're looking for in a relationship. So there are some serious things that go along with that comment.
Jack	You guys can ask questions about anything.
Johnella	Yeh, it's what we're quite good at. But without the answers it doesn't go anywhere does it?
	So anyway how would you in the group, how would we go about checking out with each other whether

	throwaway comments are just fun or whether throwaway comments have seriousness to them? Or a serious side?
Jack	I don't know. Maybe we could all just say, 'I didn't mean anything by that,' after we speak perhaps.
Johnella	What if in the group, eight people out of the nine think it's funny and one person doesn't think it's funny. They take it seriously. Do you think it would be easy in a group to say, 'I don't think it's so funny?' when eight people say, 'It's funny?'
Jack	No. Probably not.
Johnella	What would you think Jack, if we always took throwaway comments a bit seriously within the group in order to find out whether they are funny comments or not?
Jack	Will we ever get a laugh in here?
Johnella	Yes, we might discover that nine out of nine people think it's very funny.
Jack	We could try, but I think I'm going to have to be careful what I say.
Johnella	As a result of this conversation you might be thinking about what's said, rather than saying it?
Jack	Mmm. I might think about what it would be like if I had to answer all these questions again. Yeh.
Johnella	If you were thinking about, so you were holding something rather than saying something, what would you decide to hold? What sort of things might you hold back rather than speak?
Jack	Comments about women.
Johnella	Hold back comments about women. Anything else that would be held back?
Jack	Comments about sex.
Johnella	Anything else?
Jack	They're probably the big ones.
Johnella	OK. So it would be a holding back that would happen. In that holding back would that be an attempt to escape this sort of process, this sort of list of questions?
Jack	Partly.
Johnella	And what else? What else would support you to hold back in this way?
Jack	Well, if people don't know me well enough in here to work out that I don't mean anything by it. It might

	be better not to say some of that stuff. I wouldn't want to hurt anyone's feelings.
Johnella	So there's a desire to protect people, not hurt their feelings, in holding back.
Jack	Yes.
Johnella	You know when you've had that experience in the pub, you know when things have been said, have they been said by people that you think know you reasonably well?
Jack	Yeh. Sometimes.
Johnella	So knowing somebody really well doesn't necessarily protect you from these sorts of throwaway comments.
Jack	Mmm. No. Maybe not. I mean sometimes they say things and I think, 'Oh. They're a good bloke and they know me. They probably didn't mean it the way it came out.'
Johnella	So you talk yourself out of it.
Jack	Mmm. Or sometimes I just think, 'God, he's pissed. How could he say that? That's really mean.'
Johnella	Yeh. If you thought Jack, that in asking these questions I'm asking you, that the intention is to get to know what you think and feel about certain things rather than to put you on the spot and blame you for saying certain things, would it make it easier to speak? What do you think?
Jack	Mmm. It might make it easier. You're going to do this with everyone else aren't you?
Johnella	Yes.
Jack	So that would happen with everybody?
Johnella	Yes. Because that's an important part of this conversation isn't it, what you think I'm doing in asking this. If you thought I was moving into blame or judgement of you, would you let me know?
Jack	I think I'd stop answering questions, if I thought you were going to do that, I thought you were going to make a fool of me here.
Johnella	Yes. OK. So if you stopped answering the questions that would tell me that you thought there was some judgement of you or I was attempting to make a fool of you.
Jack	Mmm. Or I might just get up and go and say, 'I'm not here for this.'

Johnella	OK. I need to say there's a strong desire on my part not to do that, but I might also not notice something. I mightn't notice that a question feels like a judgemental question, or feels like a putting you on the spot question, so I'd really appreciate you telling me that. Although I'll also be noticing if you stop asking questions or answering questions. I'll notice that as well. Is that OK?
Jack	Yes.
Johnella	What I want to do now Jack, is go back to the group and just talk about these sorts of throwaway comments and the effect they might have, and how we might talk about them in the group
Jack	Mmm. Hmm.
Johnella	As a way to get to know each other. Is that OK?
Jack	Mmm. Hmm.

Throughout this prismatic dialogue, I am demonstrating the degree of persistence that is required to move taken-for-granted attitudes into focus. The textual representation of the conversation excludes a lot of relevant information, such as tone of voice, posture, hesitation and eye contact. The questions that I ask are only relevant when we take the person's responses into account, including their non-verbal responses. If I was to interview another person who made the same initial comment as Jack, the interview would be quite different.

The prioritising of some questions over others reflects the judgements that we hold. In other words, questions can orientate us (therapists and clients) either towards discovery or towards our own preconceived ideas. People's (clients') responses to the questions that we ask can also reflect their interpretations of our intentions.

Through the use of prismatic dialogue, I hope to provide therapists with the experience of noticing the effects of the judgements that they hold on the therapeutic conversations. These effects can include lecturing others, moving into silence, or hearing one comment while failing to notice another.

I mentioned earlier that the purpose of this prismatic dialogue was to create an opportunity for the counsellor to experience the effect of this enquiry. Through this dialogue Sally (the counsellor) experienced a process that would subsequently assist her to move from a place of silence to a place of meaning negotiation. Subsequent to this prismatic dialogue I would want to identify and explore the technical and emotional resources Sally would need in order to feel confident about facilitating a conversation in a similar situation.

extending the clinical edge
of the counsellor

In the next example, Lisa (counsellor) reports in super-vision that she was struggling to make use of the difference she had identified in nine year old Simon's control of 'temper' at Health camp and lack of control of 'temper' at home. In this situation we oscillate between having a conversation together and using prismatic dialogue.

Lisa	Kids will usually say something along the lines of, 'Oh. I wouldn't do that at Health camp.' When I question around that, it is because the teachers would deal with it/handle it. Then somehow it swings back to that edge that puts the blame on the parents for not being as good as the Health camp workers.
Johnella	You can take the conversation to the next step by asking questions like:

- Does that knowing that the teachers will deal with it, stop the temper building?
- How fast can you sit on the temper?
- How do you do this?
- Do you say to yourself, 'I had better not do this?'

Lisa	Put the skill back onto the child.
Johnella	We are re-searching ... What we are trying to bring forward is that the quicker we get on top of this, the less likely it is there will be an explosion. If the temper is let go, there will be an explosion! I am sure at Health camp there has been a couple of times where they have not 'got on top of it.' It is listening too. What are the first signs? Is it a grumpy feeling? Is it a grumpy voice? A 'bloody hell I'm not going to do it!' A stamping foot? What's the first sign?
Lisa	With Simon, he went into Health camp and was absolutely good as gold. He drove them mad because he wouldn't put a foot wrong. There was reportage though of bad weekends. When they asked him about it, he would smile and say he would never loose his temper at Health camp. When we talked about it, he got into the big, 'I don't knows.'

Johnella	Never lost his temper at Health camp?
Lisa	Absolutely! He knew he never would, but he would at home.
Johnella	OK. Lisa take up Simon's position for a second. Simon, how do you know that?
Simon (Lisa)	I just know.
Johnella	You just know? Is that knowing a really strong knowing? Would you say it is a really strong knowing?
Simon (Lisa)	I just know.
Johnella	Each time you go back to Health camp and this temper follows you, do you think this knowing grows?
Simon (Lisa)	Yes. It does.
Johnella	So it has got stronger as you keep going back to Health camp.
Simon (Lisa)	Yes. They keep pushing me so I know.
Johnella	Do you know when the push is happening?
Simon (Lisa)	Yes. I do.
Johnella	What tells you this push is happening?
Simon (Lisa)	The look in their eyes. I just know.
Johnella	So there is a look in their eyes that says 'a push is happening'?
Simon (Lisa)	Yes.
Johnella	When you notice this eye - this look - what do you say or do to yourself?
Simon (Lisa)	I am not going to let them push me into this.
Johnella	So you say to yourself, 'I am not going to let them push me into this'?
Simon (Lisa)	Yep. I do.
Johnella	When you hear yourself say that, is there any strength with that?
Simon (Lisa)	Yes. There is a lot of strength with that.
Johnella	There is a lot of strength with that. So there is strength and determination! I'm not going to let them push me into temper.
Simon (Lisa)	Yep. You are not going to do that to me.
Johnella	OK. So you are carrying the strength and determination back into Health camp. You would watch for that look in the eye ...
Simon (Lisa)	Yep. I've got them sussed!
Johnella	Did you know you were as determined and as strong as this?

Simon (Lisa)	No. I was pretty surprised actually. Although sometimes at school, I have shown it too.
Johnella	Lisa, what we have now is a knowledge of strength and determination. 'I see it in their eyes. I'm not going to let them do it to me. I'm going to hold on!' Now you need to re-search where does this strength and determination go when you get home?
Lisa	That's the question I don't know the answer to.

I am going to focus on strength and determination, and might ask:

Johnella	If you put aside this strength and determination at Health camp - say you said, 'Oh. I'm not going to have it today.' What would happen?
Simon (Lisa)	I would be in trouble.
Johnella	So strength and determination defend you from trouble?
Simon (Lisa)	Yes.
Johnella	Is trouble from Health camp different from trouble at home?
Simon (Lisa)	Yes.
Johnella	What's the difference?
Simon (Lisa)	In trouble at Health camp, I'm just in trouble. I don't like it. In trouble at home, it hurts.
Johnella	So trouble at home brings hurt. If you knew that you could use strength and determination - the strength and determination that you found at Health camp - if you knew that you could use that to defend yourself from this hurt - would you be interested?
Lisa	I think that he might be.
Johnella	It is interesting to me that this trouble brings about feelings of hurt at home and that trouble brings upset/ punishment at Health camp. He brings forward strength and determination at Health camp and uses it. He doesn't at home. So the wondering I have for the therapy is both: What stops him using this knowledge? And what would help him use this knowledge?

CHAPTER 2

super-vision and
experiential knowledge

In the super-vision environment, it is possible and advantageous for therapists to identify and reflect on the direct experiences that they have, by using a relational enquiry process.

Experiential knowledge is commonly shaped through direct reference to the self such as, 'What do I think/feel/experience?' and this knowledge is then expressed through conventional use of the English language. Consequently, we (therapists and clients) can take up these positions:

- I feel/think/experience this, thus it is true. You feel/think/experience something different, so you're wrong.

- I feel/think/experience this, is it true? You feel/think/experience something different, maybe I am wrong.

- I feel/think/experience this, is it true? You feel/think/experience the same, it must be true.

These positions are constructed and we (therapists and clients) use binary forms of thinking and speaking such as, 'I am frightened (or not)', 'I am right (or wrong)', 'This is true (or false).' When experience is expressed definitively such as, 'I'm frustrated/angry/hurt/silenced/

frightened', people often reflect on this position and ask, 'How did I get here? Who placed me here?' In order to answer these questions, they look around them and frequently answer, 'You did it to me/put me in this circumstance/made me do it.' In contrast, people who experience marginalisation can search for an explanation within themselves. For example, 'Maybe I did this/put myself here/made you do it.'

I regard direct experience as informing me about something, rather than as being 'true' or 'false'. I allow myself to have this experience in order to fully appreciate the experience. I can then relationally express the experience, which allows me to search for contextual meaning. Amongst other things, this search can expose the effects on the self of being 'culturally positioned as wrong or lesser than others.' I believe using relational language-making allows me to do the following

- notice the experience
- validate the experience such as, 'This is telling me something'
- relationally language the experience
- contextually re-search the experience

This process allows me to tentatively consider using direct experience for the benefit of the therapy. I believe that in relationships where there is a power relation, such as super-vision and therapy, the use of relational consciousness and relational language-making is integral to ethical use of direct experience for the benefit of the other, and the relationship.

If I experience strong emotions while meeting with another person (therapist or client), I may need to hold this experience to myself in order to protect the therapeutic or super-vision relationship. Once the session ends I can allow myself to fully experience the emotion or experience, whilst attempting to name it. I promptly move this name into relational language, which positions me to contextually explore the experience. This contextual exploration includes considering people's (clients) experience of me.

At some point in this exploration, I consider how to tentatively take this experiential knowledge back to the super-vision or therapeutic relationship. This decision is guided by the ethic of only introducing information which will benefit/support this relationship. The benefit that I am describing is determined by reflecting on each participant's ethical obligations within the bounds of this relationship.

Annabel brought this dilemma to super-vision:

Annabel	I caught myself feeling really judgemental about this woman. She is married and is simultaneously having two affairs with other men. The two lovers know about the husband, but not about each other. The husband believes the relationship to be monogamous. As you can imagine, Christine (client) is finding it difficult to juggle these relationships, including the stories she tells each person. There was a statement she made that floored me. I just felt so judgemental about it. Well, judgemental is a little mild. I felt outraged! Consequently I said something lame, and missed what I now think was a therapeutic opportunity.
Johnella	OK. Let's start with that moment. Annabel, take up Christine's position and repeat what she said.
Christine (Annabel)	I heard this radio programme and they were talking about the war in Iraq. In particular, the number of women violated and abused through war. I found myself thinking, 'That's exactly what I'm feeling. I feel out of control.' I also felt abused when Ric, my lover, took me home to meet his Mum. She was so rude to me. It was just terrible. I know it affected Ric. He sort of withdrew from me. I felt my heart was breaking.
Johnella	Christine, is this the first experience in your life where you have felt that the control in your life, lies with someone else?
Christine (Annabel)	Oh, absolutely. I never knew that it was possible to feel like this. I mean, Annabel tells me this is how other people feel with a broken heart, but I can't imagine.
Johnella	So from the time that you were quite small until this time, there's been a sense, or even an experience, that it is possible to control what happens in your life?

Christine (Annabel)	Yes. I wouldn't have even thought of it like that. You know, I would have just thought, 'Well, this is my life.'
Johnella	Like, this is normal ... Would it feel like this is everybody's life, or was this just a special life?
Christine (Annabel)	Well. I suppose you know, it's not everybody's life - but it was a pretty ordinary life. It was pretty ordinary for my friends at University, and then at work at A and E.
Johnella	So it felt pretty normal in a way?
Christine (Annabel)	Yes.
Johnella	OK. In your work, when you came across people where the control of decisions and control of well-being, both mental and physical, was in the hands of someone else's - through rape, car accidents, all sorts of things - how do you understand that experience when you look back?
Christine (Annabel)	Umm. Well, I mean, I've always been interested in the science of medicine, and I mean I want to do a good job for people. I suppose that's more the way I've seen it. I thought, 'Well. I've been doing the best I can do.'
Johnella	OK. So this is more a science approach. I wonder is this different from a type of approach where you're wondering, 'What's this like for this person?'
Christine (Annabel)	Yeah.
Johnella	Do you think is it possible Christine, that you've taken this sort of science response to these relationships, the live-in relationship and the two other relationships you are involved in?
Christine (Annabel)	No.
Johnella	Like a pragmatic ... ?
Christine (Annabel)	I think ... I mean, I wouldn't have thought. I would never have thought of that myself - but when you ask it, I think, 'Well, yes.' I mean, you know, I've settled with this guy who I mean, I who ... Umm. You know initially I was more strongly attracted to him, but I think he's much more strongly attracted to me now. You know, he's a good catch. He's a really nice person and ... Yeah. I think I just thought that I was going to have this pretty sort of normal life that

	I see all my friends having, but the older I get, the less I think that I actually want that.
Johnella	Mmm.
Christine (Annabel)	You know, when I look around at everyone else having it, now having the children, settling down, having the house ... Well, I've got the house and I don't even know if I actually want it.
Johnella	Mmm. Do you think this search is for something different? It sounds like the relationship with the person you are living with is certainly as you were describing it - had some sense of a science pragmatic approach to it, you know, 'He's a good catch. He's a nice person', it seems you were listing those sorts of qualities? Do you think in the search for something different that leads you to these two other relationships?
Christine (Annabel)	Yes. I think that it has.
Johnella	Have these two other relationships moved you away from the science pragmatic response to a more heart practice, a heart knowledge?
Christine (Annabel)	Umm. I'm not sure I know what you mean by a heart knowledge. I do feel more free, have more fun, like you know, going dancing and I'm a lot more sexual.
Johnella	OK. Christine, if you discovered that without your knowing or consent that these other two men were lying to you and had multiple other relationships, how would that feel? What feelings would that bring forward?
Christine (Annabel)	Umm. I think with one of them it wouldn't really matter as long as we were using a condom, because that really is just a sex thing. With the other guy who I have fallen in love with, that would be devastating.
Johnella	Mmm. And what would be devastating about that for you?
Christine (Annabel)	Umm. Well, I feel a bit funny saying it because he would have lied to me and I'm lying to my partner, so it doesn't feel that fair in that way, but that is how it would feel.
Johnella	So a part of the devastation would be around trust, betrayal of trust, lying, cheating?
Christine (Annabel)	Yes.

Johnella	Does the man that you're in love with, know about the other man?
Christine (Annabel)	No.
Johnella	So what you're doing is a betrayal of trust to the love he has for you?
Christine (Annabel)	I suppose you could put it like that.
Johnella	In saying that, in this relationship have you considered that in this relationship there is a search for something different? A search for something different beyond the scientific pragmatic response. You are engaging the heart, you say, you feel 'in love' with this man.
Christine (Annabel)	Yes.
Johnella	Did it start off maybe in a pragmatic sexual way?
Christine (Annabel)	Yes.
Johnella	Now it's come to this. When you think about that love, you said that devastation would follow if you felt that there had been lying and betrayal in this relationship.
Christine (Annabel)	Yes.
Johnella	And now, as you answer this question, are you now thinking that this devastation could be experienced by him?
Christine (Annabel)	Yes.
Johnella	If that devastation was experienced by him, where would that leave the relationship that you have with him?
Christine (Annabel)	Umm. I can hardly bear to think about it actually. It would be all pretty messy.
Johnella	In the messiness, would you have any control over the outcome do you believe?
Christine (Annabel)	Umm. Oh. I don't think so. I mean, I just don't think I want to go there. I mean, he knows I still have sex from time to time with my regular partner, but I think the other guy would be too much for him.
Johnella	So there is this search for something different that you've been pursuing. This search has taken you beyond the scientific pragmatic response. There are some things that have happened and could happen, that would leave you without the experience of control, such as

	your partner finding out that there had been betrayal of trust.
Christine (Annabel)	Yes.
Johnella	Do you think you carry a lot of life practice in being out of control in this way? In any way?
Christine (Annabel)	No. I've never struck anything like this before.
Johnella	Mmm. I wonder if this lack of practice has actually stopped you from thinking about the things that you need to do to protect yourself, and to also protect these relationships. When you were saying to me that you loved this man yet you, 'Didn't even want to go there. If he discovered this betrayal of trust, it would be devastating.'
Christine (Annabel)	Mmm.
Johnella	Knowing this, what strategies can you use to protect this relationship?
Christine (Annabel)	I think that's the thing. I don't know whether I really want to do anything anyway. Even though I feel that I have fallen in love with him at the moment. I mean, I fell in love with the man I live with, and this is how it is with him after all these years. Maybe that's just how it goes. And so I just think, '... Mmm, do I really ... ?' You know sometimes I think, 'Oh. Yes. I really want to be with him. I want to fall in love. I want to spend my life with him.' And other times I think, 'No. In ten years I'm just going to be in the same place, so I may as well just stay in the same place, just have these affairs and maybe I'll just always have affairs.'
Johnella	OK. So are you prepared then emotionally and in all sorts of ways, to deal with 'the devastation' that either comes when he finds out - or comes when you find out - that someone that you have a love relationship with has betrayed that trust? Are you prepared for that devastation?
Christine (Annabel)	Well. You know I would like to say, 'No,' but when I look at what I'm doing I think the answer has to be, 'Yes.'
Johnella	OK.
Christine (Annabel)	Because you know, I am still sleeping with both of the other guys and my partner, while the man

	I love is talking to his family about whether we can be together.
Johnella	OK. So the choice that you are making at the moment is to court devastation, to court the potential for devastation. Up until this moment this devastation has mostly been avoided. Except for the family upset.
Christine (Annabel)	Yes. Well ... Yeah. I think I can see it's risky what I'm doing, but I don't really seem to be ready to give any of it up at the moment.
Johnella	OK. You know that you are prepared to court the potential for devastation. That's a decision that's been made by you. From a counselling point of view, I wouldn't say, 'You mustn't do that ... ' I mean we talked about the possible consequences and maybe this is part of this search for a new direction - to court the potential for devastation.
Christine (Annabel)	Yes. I mean it's a lot to think about. I suppose I just prefer not to go there really, but ... Umm ... I can see ... You know ... It is a risk, what I am doing.
Johnella	OK. Let's finish here. I want to talk to Annabel.
	Annabel, in this interview Christine moved away from comparing the experience she was having to that of rape victims. She appears to have had limited life experiences of powerlessness and many life experiences of 'control'. I suspect the pain she is experiencing is so foreign, she is grappling to make sense of this. You can see that when we stay with the experience she's having, rather than judging this experience, Christine moves to a place of agency, 'I would prefer to court the potential for devastation.' At this point, she is in a position to consider the living out of this decision either through counselling or directly in her life.

If I had discovered through this process that the response Annabel had reflected an issue she was having in her life, then this issue would be taken up in super-vision. This discussion is oriented towards exploring ways of liberating the therapy from this limitation. Occasionally we identify that the therapist would benefit from a more intensive engagement with the issue. In these instances, I suggest the therapist explores the issue outside super-vision with a therapist. Whenever therapists struggle to collaboratively contextualise an experience, this can alert us to the appearance of a judgement, value or theoretical position that is limiting exploration. I think super-vision is the ideal venue for exploring this struggle.

One of the indicators that an issue, judgement or belief has moved to a more settled place is a change in the emotional quality of the therapist's experience. This is achieved as therapists find multiple ways to make sense of experience, and in turn constructs the space for people (clients) to discover 'the sense' that works for their lives.

introducing possibilities
through using tentative language

Once I determine that a response or reaction I have is relevant to the super-vision relationship, I introduce this experience as a tentative possibility using expressions such as, 'Could it be ...' or 'Is it something like ...?' I do this by making a statement that incorporates using relational language followed by questioning. I might say, for example,

> Whenever I suggest a possibility for the counselling, I notice that you frequently respond with a statement like, "It seems so obvious, I'll never get this." Do you notice this? I'm a little worried that this super-vision may be reducing the sense of competence or confidence you have in the work. How do you think I can contribute to the work you do without it being experienced as evidence of being *right* or *wrong*?

Transparency is an incomplete description of what I do. I prefer to describe it as taking a *tentative* approach to the naming of experience, which I then relationally express and contextually re-search. Out of session I consider if and how the experiential metaphor that I have developed could be used for the benefit of the relationship (Note 14). Any assumed benefit can be negotiated directly with the person using relational language, and any assumed disadvantages can be explored in a super-vision/consultation process.

re-searching experience by taking up the inside/outside position

The inside/outside position is generated in super-vision through this process:

➡ I ask the therapist to express in an uncensored way the feelings, experiences or thoughts she/he has about the therapeutic relationship and the people in this relationship.

➡ I listen to this expression and extract the significant themes, feelings and/or ideas.

➡ I then move these themes, feelings and/or ideas into relational language.

➡ I facilitate a contextual exploration of these themes, feelings and/ or ideas.

diagram 2: the insider/outsider experience

insider experience internalised language	insider/outsider experience relational language-making
I'm so frustrated with him.	The frustration you felt, when did you first notice this?

Once I have generated relational language, I can engage in a contextual exploration of this experience. This contextual exploration can include the therapist's life experiences, the experience within the therapeutic relationship and the expectation that people (therapist and client) hold of the therapy. In the same super-vision session, I might ask the therapist to take up the position of the client. I do this in order to demonstrate alternative possibilities for exploration, and provide the therapist with experiential knowledge resources.

Throughout this process, I can acknowledge that the insider experience. 'I felt silenced when Jack (client) demanded we change direction', is telling us something that we need to listen to and understand. However new possibilities only become apparent as we relationally and contextually explore this direct experience. Once we identify these new possibilities, we can then review how to tentatively take these possibilities back to the therapeutic relationship. I am emphasising the *tentative* nature of this knowledge, in order to keep the focus on discovery.

The inside/outside position allows us to notice how the conversation and the relationship is impacting on us. This impact can be identified through thoughts, feelings, body responses and the ability to stay in the present moment. When we bring our awareness to these responses, we can experiment with finding a tentative name for the experience, at the same time considering its relevance to the super-vision or therapeutic relationship.

We may decide it is important to immediately use this experience to directly negotiate the parameters of the relationship. Therapists who are interested in collaborative approaches can talk themselves out of experiences of discomfort, and consequently experience a degree of powerlessness. This can occur when people (clients) are taking strong positions in relationship to the therapist, or in relationship to a partner or child, such as, 'I want you (the therapist) to tell me what to do,' or 'I want an equal relationship,' or 'Tell me about your (therapist's) life,' or 'I want to stop counselling and become your friend.'

In super-vision, I use prismatic dialogue to demonstrate ways to respond to these situations. At the same time, through the prismatic dialogue, the therapist experiences this response from the position of the person (client). In the two examples below, I am using prismatic dialogue to provide therapists with an opportunity to negotiate experience in the present moment.

 prismatic dialogue

Ana (therapist)	I totally lost my way in this couple session. I felt I couldn't get a word in. Roberta and Craig started arguing as soon as they sat down.
Johnella	Let's experiment with ways to negotiate the direction of the conversation.
	Roberta and Craig, I'd like you to stop for a moment. There has been a lot of anger directed toward each other today. Is there anything new that you have discovered through talking this way? I'd like to suggest a different way of talking

	for the rest of the session. Are you interested in that?
Ana	I can see how I could use this at the beginning of the session. The thing that worried me most about the last session was that toward the end Craig got louder and louder. I felt I began to placate him. I was worried that the situation was getting out of hand. I felt I'd totally lost control - but then if I had taken control, isn't that disrespectful to him?
Johnella	Can you take up the position of Craig for a moment?
	Craig, the anger you are expressing seems to be escalating. I'd like to reduce the level of this anger as I don't think this is a useful way to have a conversation. We could take a break or you could go for a walk. Do you have other ideas that would assist you in reducing this anger?

prismatic dialogue

Stephen (therapist)	Carlos started to withdraw as we talked about his relationship with his dad. I found myself talking into a void. He said nothing. He kept his head down. I just kept asking questions and telling stories. By the end of the session, I felt exhausted and I thought I'd lost him. I'm really nervous about the next session.
Johnella	Can you recall what the two of you were saying prior to the moment where you thought he withdrew from the conversation?
Stephen	He was talking about the different treatment each brother got from the dad.
Johnella	What did he say?
Stephen	It was something like, 'He had standards and you had to go along with him or else. Though Ben was always let off easy.'
Johnella	Stephen, take up Carlos' position for a minute.
	Carlos, last week I noticed that as you began to talk about 'the different standards' and the different treatment of Ben, 'He was let off easy,'

	you moved into silence. When this occurred, I responded by talking more, asking questions, telling stories. Did you notice this? If I had sat with you in the silence, what would that have been like for you? Were there feelings that you were experiencing in this silence?'
Johnella	Or I could say, 'Carlos, I've noticed that after I spoke, the room felt very still. We have also begun to talk very quietly. Have you noticed this?'
Carlos (Stephen)	Yes. I'm feeling a little low.
Johnella	When did you notice the feeling level change?'

The inside/outside position assists me to be both in the therapeutic/ super-vision relationship, while re-viewing the impact of being in the relationship. When I use this position I can more readily

- catch myself before or after I have subjected people to an imposition of meaning
- use present-moment experience as a knowledge resource for the relationship
- challenge binary oppositions by taking up an inside/outside place (Bird 2000, pp 140-166)

  Binary thinking results in either

  - over-involvement
    (where the feelings, thinking or experiences that I have are considered either true or dismissed)
  - over-detachment
    (where I believe I am acting as a neutral observer)

In the two diagrams following, I am demonstrating the importance of noticing and then tentatively naming the experiences I have, while at the same time holding back from expressing these experiences to the person (client). I hold the expression until I understand how I can use this for the benefit of the therapy.

The first diagram illustrates the way in which I use the direct experiences that I have in therapeutic or super-vision relationships. The second shows the process that I use when unsure about the relevance to the therapeutic or super-vision relationship of an experience that I am having.

diagram 3: working with the inside/outside experience
in the present moment

Notice a feeling, thought, body sensation or experience.	Tentatively name this experience to yourself, while reviewing the relevance of it to the present moment therapeutic conversation. If the experience belongs to your life, hold the experience. Explore this in super-vision.	If the experience appears relevant to this relationship, ask a question using relational language. The intention is to negotiate meaning by raising a possibility.	Act to support the therapeutic or super-vision relationship.
		For example, *I noticed a degree of tension in the conversation after I asked if the letter I sent you had been useful in any way. After that, you talked about the recent conflict at work, and I moved the conversation back to the letter. I'm left wondering which topic is most relevant for you - the letter or the conflict at work? I'm also wondering if it is easy or hard to speak about any limitations or inaccuracies you might have experienced in the letter?*	For example, *I will remain alert to any indication that you have moved away from the conversation into a disconnected place. I'd also be interested in discovering what would tell you that you have started to move away from the conversation. How could you alert me to this?*

diagram 4: holding the experience in the present moment

Notice a feeling, thought, body sensation or experience.

Tentatively name this experience to yourself. Hold the experience, in order to explore it contextually outside of the therapy. Through this exploration in super-vision (including prismatic dialogue), it will become possible to determine how to use this experience responsibly and therapeutically.

When the experience belongs principally to your life, you act to protect the therapy from imposition. When the experience can be used to benefit the therapy, you use relationship language to negotiate meaning.

Act to support the therapeutic or super-vision relationship.

👫 prismatic dialogue

In this example, Katy (therapist) described a statement that Claire (client) had made.

Claire   I'm only interested in a relationship if Robbie has got insight.

Katy felt burdened by this statement. She noticed she felt responsible for 'giving Robbie insight.' So she brought this to super-vision.

Johnella   Yes. So I might begin by saying, 'What do you think Claire, when you talk about wanting a sense of insight? What are you talking about? What would give you a sense of insight?'

Katy   She would say, 'A sense of insight which meets me somewhere in the needs I have.'

Johnella   OK. Take up Claire's position Katy.
Now Claire, in that process of meeting you somewhere, if I was to say to you that it may take some time for us to negotiate that process together, would that surprise you? Are you expecting the insight to happen today?

Claire (Katy) I know that it will take time.

Johnella   OK. So while it takes time to find out whether Robbie is prepared to meet you somewhere, what would tell you that a sense of impatience was growing around waiting for Robbie to meet you somewhere? Let's say after this session, if you felt that the meeting process had moved things, but you'd hoped it would move things further - what would you find yourself doing or saying?

Claire (Katy) I don't want to put a lot of hope into this. I just have a little bit of my life back.

Johnella   So you are going to give this conversational process limited hope?

Claire (Katy) Yes. I don't want ever to be going back to this feeling of self loathing, because I couldn't stand the frustration.

Johnella   And do you think that the limited hope will help you to take the time that you need and Robbie needs to see if this relationship can work?

Claire (Katy)	I need to see some evidence, step by step ... I'm prepared to wait.
Johnella	OK. Good. Could you let me know if you felt that things were either moving too fast for you or too slow for you?
Claire (Katy)	Yes. I could do that.
Johnella	Because that's also what I want to check with Robbie.
Claire (Katy)	Yes.
Johnella	Can you take up the position of Robbie please?

In the prismatic dialogue above, I am demonstrating a process in which Claire (Katy) is positioned to alert me to the discoveries she is making in respect to Robbie's 'insight'. This process will hopefully act to lift the burden off the therapist.

Therapists often need to hold onto their initial experience, rather than directly express this experience to people (clients). The therapist does this in order to determine how relevant this experience is to the super-vision or therapeutic conversation.

Even when I consider the experience is relevant, such as feeling anger at an injustice, I may still experiment with ways to express this experience outside of the session. I do this in order to protect the therapeutic relationship from an interpretation that could be limiting such as, 'Johnella was so affected by my description of the abuse, I won't tell her the rest. Why should anyone else have to carry these memories!'

Sometimes the strong feelings we have - such as distress or joy - can be acknowledged, while the meaning that people make of this is also explored.

 prismatic dialogue

Connie brought the following issue to super-vision:

Connie (therapist) I found myself getting quite tearful as Jackie described her experience with her family. She had gone away on a walking trip with friends. It was the first time she had spent a night away from home since the rape. We had done a lot of preparation for the trip. Jackie felt acknowledged by the group as competent and organised. She

	had fun as well as adventure. When she went home, family members were dismissive and uninterested in the weekend events. Jackie's mood plummeted and she began to talk about the weekend as though it was nothing. I feel worried about my tears. Was it appropriate or not?
Johnella	Connie, take up the position of Jackie.
	Jackie, you may have noticed I was tearful as you described the devastation you experienced when family members showed limited interest in the profound and joyful experience you had on the weekend. What did you make of these tears? Did this limit or hinder you in any way?
Jackie (Connie)	I was surprised. It took me back. I thought to myself maybe it was OK that I felt upset with my family. What do you think about what happened?
Johnella	The tears were mixed. I thought the weekend sounded amazing. It was a major accomplishment to spend a night away from home where you experienced acknowledgement from others and had fun at the same time. There were tears for this, and tears for the limited ability that family members demonstrated to celebrate this with you. Does this answer your question?

Whenever I think that a present moment experience of mine could dominate the conversation, I know I have stepped or could step, into an insider position. To act from this insider position contravenes the therapeutic or super-vision relationship understanding I work within. Instead, I ask myself to notice the experience while holding the expression of this experience.

🎎 dialogue

In this next fragment of conversation, Eve and I were tempted to talk together in super-vision about Todd's position. If this had continued, Eve and I would have simply remained mystified and perhaps judgemental about Todd's viewpoint. This was challenged through the development of a question.

Eve	Linda (Tod's partner) was stunned because she hadn't known he'd separated emotionally two years ago. So when she came to the next

	session, we reviewed this and the impact of it. It was an interesting conversation because for him, nothing had changed. Even after this statement, he was still thinking that even though it wasn't the best relationship ever, they could go on living together.
Johnella	You talked about living together.
Eve	Living together. And of course, he still expected sex. He had continued to have sex even though he had separated emotionally.
Johnella	That's amazing after two years of disconnection. What I think is fascinating is ... if he was in the room and you said, 'You have disconnected your heart from this relationship for two years, and there is still an expectation that with a disconnected heart that you can still have sex ... What sort of sex is this?' What would he say?

At the point where Eve said, 'And of course he still expected sex', and I responded, 'That's amazing after two years of disconnection', we could have easily slid into a position of assuming and agreeing that this expectation was unreasonable.

However I caught this assumption, and explored the link between the expectation for sex and the statement that Todd had made earlier, 'Two years ago, I emotionally disconnected from Linda.' The question I asked that ended with, 'What sort of sex is this?' created the opportunity for Todd to explore the answer including the context that supported his answer. At the same time, Eve and I were positioned to make a discovery that might shift or alter the assumptions that we held. This therapeutic opportunity would have been absent, if Eve and I had maintained our position or conclusion.

CHAPTER 3

prioritising the therapist

I think a central component of super-vision is encouraging therapists to be aware of the possible effect on them of engaging in therapeutic conversations. These include:

- The physical effect on our bodies as we sit very still. This stillness is particularly present as we attend closely to another's description of past traumatic experiences.

- The experiential response to another's account of a situation. These experiences may include fear, anxiety, compassion, connection, revulsion, anger, joy or judgement.

- The effect of holding an experiential response in order to explore its usefulness to the therapeutic relationship.

- The effect over time of the requirement to extend availability to others regardless of the life demands being made on the therapist.

These effects become more apparent through using prismatic dialogue. Prismatic dialogue assists us to expose presuppositions, connect with subjective experiences and experiment with a conversational direction that illuminates contradictions and dilemmas, rather than resolves them. This dialogue can involve an exploration of those subjective experiences that become visible as we take up each part of the therapeutic relationship.

Now I would like to discuss the boundary that surrounds the super-vision relationship, explore a process to reconnect with feelings and experiences, and then look at the use of direct experience in skill development.

the boundary that surrounds the professional and the personal

Super-vision relationships, like therapeutic relationships, are bound by a negotiated understanding that include

- each person's responsibilities in regard to the relationship, such as professional, ethical and institutional requirements

- the time allocated for the relationship

- the power relation inherent in the relationship. This requires participants to negotiate the possible effects of this power relation in other settings, such as jointly participating in professional events

- the ability to negotiate the limits of any exploration of personal issues

I prefer to negotiate the super-vision/consultation understanding at the beginning of the relationship, then review it annually. The boundary that surrounds the super-vision relationship defines the type of relationship we are in. This description may sound simple and perhaps commonplace. However the way this relationship is perceived generates real effects. I believe the idea of a boundary that surrounds us, rather than sits between us, allows us to

- acknowledge the real effects of being in this relationship, while reviewing how to use these effects for the benefit of the relationship

- bring ourselves to the relationship, while acknowledging the power relation inherent in the relationship

- discuss the maintenance of the boundary that surrounds us, including each person's contribution to this

- negotiate the effect on the relationship of one person's behaviour or actions. This is particularly pertinent when the super-vision/

consultation relationship understanding is threatened by either participant's behaviour

- negotiate both the progress of the relationship and the ending of the relationship

Generating this boundary creates the possibility that one person can meet another person in a collaborative enterprise. The boundary also has the effect of allowing and encouraging us to bring a connected presence to the super-vision/consultation endeavour. In turn, a connected sense of presence allows us to notice the relational environment within which we are immersed.

I may notice an experience or feeling that I am having in this relationship. In order to use this experience or feeling, I need to consider how this will benefit or fit within the bounds of the super-vision/consultation relationship. I can tentatively name this experience, while considering the appropriateness of this name, by using a relational enquiry.

In other words, I can attend to subjective direct experience, then tentatively name this experience to myself, while positioning it within the relational context. The name I have ascribed to the experience may change or remain the same. I can then form a question using relational language. The intention of the question is to use direct experience to develop and negotiate consensual meaning within the bounds of the understanding of the super-vision/consultation relationship.

I noticed, for example, that while Lex struggled to articulate her concerns about her clinical work, she found it easy to speak about what was working well. Whenever I responded to a concern, Lex typically said, 'I did that,' or 'I asked that question.' This response closed down any conversation about possibilities. Consequently super-vision was limited. This realisation led me to represent what I had noticed to Lex by asking:

➡ Do you think hearing something new in any way represents a lack or failure in you as a therapist?

➡ Have you ever learnt something new and felt supported in this learning?

➡ When I present an idea, suggestion or question, do you find yourself thinking, 'How would the person I'm working with respond?' or do you find yourself thinking, 'Have I asked something like that?'

➡ How could I present ideas, suggestions or questions in ways that support you to hold a sense of competence or confidence?

Although all the participants in the relationship can be active in discussing and supporting the bounds of the relationship, I believe the person holding institutional and relational power has particular responsibilities including

· holding an awareness of the bounds of this relationship

· reflecting and reviewing the effect of these bounds on the individuals and on the relationship

· undertaking to maintain these bounds for the benefit of the relationship

Ruth, for example, worked in a small rural community. She regularly discussed with people (clients) the implications of say, meeting at the supermarket or at the school. Ruth brought to super-vision a situation with which she felt she needed assistance. She was presently negotiating the end of a therapeutic relationship which had been significant for both participants. Ruth identified that through this therapeutic relationship she had discovered much about the subtleties of working with traumatic injuries. Clara (the client) identified that Ruth had created a safe environment that made it possible to challenge shame, and speak what previously had remained private.

Clara and Ruth were similar in age, ethnicity and had children of a same age. Clara broached the topic of moving the therapeutic relationship into a friendship. The way she did this was to comprehensively argue for this possibility. Ruth found herself almost speechless through fear of offending Clara. Internally, she was going through an ethical argument while weighing up her subjective experience. When Clara proposed meeting next week for coffee, Ruth said she needed to think about this further and signalled that she would discuss it in super-vision.

In super-vision we can discuss, clarify and state the ethical guidelines that professional groups follow. I also prefer that therapists experience and reflect on the complexity of the power relationship in therapy (⬜Note 15). Consequently I asked Ruth these questions:

➡ Ruth, how does the style of relating that has evolved within the bounds of the therapeutic relationship affect your ability to centralise the needs you have while reflecting on Clara's request?

➡ The nature of therapeutic relationships requires you to prioritise the other person (in this instance Clara) whenever you meet together. How is this similar or different to the way you prioritise people in friendships?

➡ What does Clara know about your life that would indicate that a mutual friendship is possible?

➡ Has any sense of obligation to support Clara's well-being impacted on the response you made to this request?

➡ Are you searching for new friendships in your life?

➡ How possible is it to say 'Yes' to this request for friendship when this request is made in the context of therapy?

➡ Does a 'Yes' or a 'No' carry the same weight?

➡ Reflect hypothetically on the possibility of a friendship with Clara. How possible would it be for you to prioritise the other relationships in your life even when Clara signalled a need of any sort? For example, choosing to delay responding to a phone call.

➡ If you were to give fifty per cent friendship availability rather than one hundred per cent therapeutic relationship availability to a conversation with Clara, how do you think she would make sense of that?

At the end of this discussion Ruth identified that she had felt unable to immediately say 'No' to Clara's request. She was worried Clara would experience this as a rejection. The knowledge she had of Clara's early life highlighted the possibility that declining Clara's proposal could result in Clara adding this onto a chorus of other disappointments and rejections in her life.

Ruth and I then engaged in a prismatic dialogue to illustrate the type of conversational process that could illuminated this complexity for Clara, while protecting the integrity of the therapeutic relationship. Subsequently, Ruth and Clara were able to reflect on and negotiate the complexity of being in a dynamic therapeutic relationship.

Then Clara negotiated a way that she could catch up with Ruth from time to time. This involved contacting and meeting Ruth at work. Ruth and Clara agreed these meetings would be an extension of the therapeutic relationship, rather than the development of a friendship. Although Ruth was responsible for maintaining this boundary, Clara indicated a willingness to participate in caretaking the boundary too.

reconnecting with feelings and experiences

Prismatic dialogue provides us with a useful vehicle to reconnect with those experiences which have been held for a week or two, rather than expressed. In therapeutic relationships we often hold back our experiences in order to protect people (clients) from imposition. We may intellectually recall the event, but struggle to reconnect with the memory of the emotional and physical experience.

Prismatic dialogue allows us to access this experience, because the conversational process uses embodied language. Reconnecting with this experience can be important for both the therapy and our health. I believe our health can suffer when we habitually hold strong emotional responses, then lose an embodied awareness of the events that generated these responses.

 dialogue

Lee (therapist) and I explore the experience she had in a prismatic dialogue.

Johnella   I wanted to have this conversation, so we could discuss what I call 'standing on the bounds' of inside/outside of direct experience. When I ask people to engage in prismatic dialogue, I believe that inside/outside boundary is moveable. It's not rigid. People move into inside-direct experience, then outside of direct experience, and then back to the inside/outside place.

When some people who attended my workshops looked at the video in which you represented Fran, one of the things they noticed was the degree of distress you experienced as you represented the experiences she had.

Some people found that distress understandable, given you were representing her experience around the death of her child. Others used terms like 'counter-transference'. That was the strongest psychological term used. Other people thought that perhaps you were touching on something personal, something that had occurred in your life.

	I responded to people's observations by saying that I believed as you took up an imaginative position in respect to Fran's experience, you were free to engage with this experience differently than you could as a therapist in the therapeutic relationship. However I wanted to give you the opportunity to also speak to this.
Lee	I guess I have got mixed feelings about these reflections. In particular, the fact that some people have watched the video and have already interpreted what I am doing and feeling!
	I guess what stands out for me in the prismatic dialogue/consultation process was that it was an enormous relief for me to know that I felt as strongly as I did. I was relieved to discover that to some extent, I carried an emotional understanding of what it was like for Fran to live in her day-to-day.
	In the therapy itself, I felt I had to hold such a particular line around supporting her emotionally, while at the same time understanding what it's like for her. I needed to do this in order to access questions and develop areas of enquiry that created new possibilities for her. She's a very intelligent woman, very onto it. There is no room to move into generalisations or platitudes. It's very strong work to manage all of that.
	Consequently, I think that what was a relief for me in the interview, was realising that I did carry a really good emotional understanding of what it was like for Fran because I had worried a bit that I hadn't. I mean it's not that I haven't had tears in my eyes from time to time. But the depth of the feeling, despair and grief that she has in the minute to minute of daily life, you know. You know, I've never shown it to her or to myself and yet ...
Johnella	That's what interests me. Is there something required of you in this work that means that you didn't show this or become aware of the experience of distress until the prismatic dialogue?
Lee	I had always carried a hope that I had an awareness. But because I had never directly experienced that degree of distress, I worried that I had become - or might become - detached.

Johnella	OK.
Lee	So then during the interview I realised I wasn't detached, I did carry a reasonable understanding of what it's emotionally like for Fran.
Johnella	Yes.
Lee	And the distress, I managed it appropriately in the room.
Johnella	Yes. When you moved into a more subjective place as you represented Fran, did you have a different appreciation about what you were needing to hold every time you saw her?
Lee	I had a different appreciation of how much I juggle in the sessions, but there was also a degree of relaxation. I know now I know enough.
Johnella	Is it that you now know imaginatively that you can go as close to somebody else's experience as is possible, given you haven't had the direct experience.
Lee	Yes. I feel confident now that when I sit with Fran, even though there aren't floods of tears or overt emotional expression, that somewhere and somehow I carry an understanding - and a growing understanding - of the experience she has. You know. Just because it's not being outwardly expressed, it's still there. I feel I've been able to breathe easier in the work .
Johnella	That's interesting.
Lee	I'm more relaxed. I just feel confident that I'm emotionally connected. Because I don't have children, and I've never lost a child, that was another big question for me, 'Did I have enough understanding to work effectively with Fran?'
Johnella	It raises an interesting question for me as you talk about the doubts you had, 'Maybe I was too detached.' People tend to know when they've crossed into the insider place because they think the other's experience is their experience. They are crying their own tears. I would hope most people know when they've crossed into the insider place.
	However I am interested in what informs counsellors that they are standing balanced in the outside/ inside place. Without the third place, the inside/ outside place, people either take up the insider place or the outside place. That was a question you

	were raising for yourself, 'Maybe I'm too detached.' The prismatic dialogue and that experience of the dialogue allowed you to answer this question, 'I'm actually on that inside/outside line.'
Lee	Yes. That I'm on that line. As I said earlier, because Fran is the sort of person she is and questions enormously, there's no place for her to rest in philosophical or religious beliefs. Consequently there is an endless questioning that requires an intellectual rigour, as well as emotional presence.
	So it is just nice for me to feel - or to know now - that I can bring both to the conversation. I'm just thinking about when you talked about the insider/outsider position. If I am moved to tears in a session, can these tears not be on behalf of another?
Johnella	Yes, they can.
Lee	Without me moving into my own grief?
Johnella	Yes. I think when people looked at that video-tape, it was the extent of the sadness. The sadness came quite quickly in the interview process. You quickly took up Fran's position so the emotions also came quite quickly.
	I suspect people were wondering how they would deal with this similar situation. Whenever we express tears, I'm interested in knowing what provoked the tears, who or what these tears are for, and how will the person makes sense of them.
Lee	Yes.
Johnella	In thinking about the process of prismatic dialogue. It is quite hard to answer that question, 'Who are these tears for?' For example, if you had shown Fran the tears you expressed in the prismatic dialogue, she may have found it overwhelming in the therapy.
Lee	Totally overwhelming. She had actually experienced feeling overwhelmed when a previous counsellor, who specialised in grief counselling, displayed distress.
Johnella	I think that's what people need to understand about the prismatic dialogue. The other thing I was interested in is what Fran made of the tears you shed as she watched the video-tape. Or she may not have commented.

Lee	I'm not sure that she commented, because I think she spoke generally of feeling really understood by me and by you, and how vital our sessions are. That's something I'll have to ask her. I don't know. There is something about people's comments, or interpretation around counter-transference and transference, that I feel really irritated about. I feel like it's been such hard work holding that line in the sessions, while imagining people's lives.
Johnella	I think people who have seen the video-tape are puzzled. I have often said in workshops that there is always language for over-involvement or over-connection, while there is no language for over-detachment. I believe over-detachment is considered a preferred professional position. Consequently people who watched the video-tape are struggling to make sense of this. Where does it fit in the therapy or counselling model they're using?
Lee	I knew Fran was going to watch the prismatic dialogue. Consequently I know if I used theoretical words to describe her experience, rather than trying to remember the words she actually used, she would have experienced that as a betrayal. To not cry would be a betrayal of her as well.
Johnella	Well ...
Lee	I'm not saying I made myself cry.
Johnella	No. But I think the crying, it says something about the relationship with Fran. It says something about the position you took up. Some people might not cry.
Lee	Might speak it. They might say, 'I'm incredibly sad.'
Johnella	Yes, and that may be very congruent with who they are. I think that some people's ability to connect with an outward expression of sadness is stronger than others. I think we have a way of thinking culturally about tears. It's possible that some counsellors watching the video may coherently represent this person's experience, without expressing tears. I think a lot of people's (therapists') feelings and experiences within the therapeutic context are pathologised. The tears are pathologised. The lack of tears are pathologised.

Lee	That's what I felt. When people use a transference/ counter-transference explanation, and see this as, 'This is where you're stuck', then I just feel absolutely misunderstood.
Johnella	I think that for years there has been a limited emphasis on developing the imaginative ability of therapists. Instead therapists have been required to intellectually know those broad categories of life experience, such as the effect on family members of parental separation. As a result of neglecting the imagination, there has been a limited conversation around the ethical bounds that support the use of the imagination.
Lee	I think - and it's probably not part of this conversation - but the capacity to imagine other people's experience occurs, as people talk. I create a movie in my mind. The talk goes into a visual story line, not a auditory one. So as I was being interviewed as Fran, I could plug into that video-tape. It feels like I can turn on a movie.
Johnella	That's interesting.
Lee	That's not flashbacks! I'm talking about a highly developed capacity to integrate and hold emotionally complex information.
Johnella	This is again something that is not really talked or spoken about as a requirement for the work.

It is difficult to textually represent the fluidity generated through prismatic dialogue. This movement is made possible through considering that the words we use are close - rather than exact - representations of actual direct experience. This attitude supports us to extract significant everyday metaphors, and move these into relational expressions in order to then experience the words again through the act of speaking. In turn, this experience is noticed, languaged into existence and woven into the fabric of relational meaning (Note 16).

I have attempted to represent this movement through the description 'inside/outside' direct experience. Standing on the inside/outside line occurs when we notice inside/direct experience, 'I'm nervous', while moving to contextually and relationally re-search it. Using this process increases our awareness of the impact of life stressors on our physical, emotional and spiritual health.

I believe super-vision can play a vital role in supporting therapists to identify these stressors. Conducting check-list reviews of therapists' well-being is better than nothing. However many of us have developed endurance strategies of which we are no longer aware. Asking us to categorise our well-being in binary oppositions such as, 'Are you OK or not?', 'Well or not?', 'Coping or not?' will mostly produce affirmative responses. In contrast, prismatic dialogue allows us to engage subjectively with the effect of therapeutic experiences on our sense of well-being.

In the prismatic dialogue above, Lee discovered that she had held back the expression of the direct experiences she was having. She reconnected with this experience as she relationally expressed and explored the imagined experience of Fran. She made discoveries about the therapy through experiencing the movement from held - and perhaps forgotten - experiences, to reconnecting with memory through embodied experiences.

Participating in this prismatic dialogue allowed Lee to step away from protecting the relationship from an imposition of meaning. From this place, she could allow herself to embrace the subjective experience, while we relationally researched the experience. The discoveries we made could then be taken back to the therapy as possibilities. The tentative nature of these possibilities is maintained through an emphasis on questions rather than statements.

Lee also talked about 'plugging into a video-tape', highlighting a visual representation of experience that guides the development of a question. This question represents a possibility that only comes to life through the person's response to the question.

prioritising relational presence through super-vision

One of the key strategies that I use to develop a resource-orientated interview is prioritising and constructing relational presence (Bird, 2004. pp 63-78). When I form a question that orientates the enquiry toward re-searching what is relationally present rather than absent, people *feel* rather than hear this difference. This occurs because we are highlighting the spoken words used by the person (client) such as,

Ricky	I lack control.
Therapist	Have you ever felt a degree of control in ...?

It is relatively easy for therapists to understand the distinction between descriptions of absence and relational presence. However it is difficult for therapists to notice the habitual use of absence descriptions of experience. Using prismatic dialogue in super-vision provides the therapist with an opportunity to notice and feel the difference generated through a relational presence enquiry.

In the past for example, Robert had seen a number of therapists about anxiety, panic attacks, and difficulty in 'committing to relationships'. Five years ago, he had discovered that his cousins had been sexually abused by their father. He had spent a lot of time at his cousins' home and wondered if he had also been sexually abused. He had significant memory gaps in respect to his childhood, and no memory of being sexually assaulted. In the fifth session, Robert reported feeling discouraged, and frightened that he might remember the abuse.

ᴉᴉ prismatic dialogue

Caroline raised this situation in super-vision. She felt herself oscillating between an exploration of this situation with Robert, and intervening by using prescriptive psychological guidelines and explanations. I asked her to enter a prismatic dialogue with me.

Robert (Caroline)	Nothing ever changes.
Johnella	If you felt something had changed, what would be different?
Robert (Caroline)	I wouldn't be overwhelmed with the feelings.
Johnella	If the feelings were manageable, what would change?
Robert (Caroline)	I'd be doing everyday things OK.
Johnella	What are the everyday things you'd be doing?
Robert (Caroline)	I'd be able to do my job without getting irritated.
Johnella	How often are you able to do the job without irritation?
Robert (Caroline)	Most of the time.
Johnella	Most of the time you are in control of the irritation?
Robert (Caroline)	Yes.
Johnella	When you think that 'most of the time these feelings are manageable,' how does this impact on the belief that 'nothing ever changes'?
Robert (Caroline)	Well. I suppose things have changed. It just doesn't feel like that somehow.

Johnella	If you could hold onto the memory that things have changed, how would that feel?
Robert (Caroline)	It would feel great.
Johnella	How does this conversation feel at the moment?
Robert (Caroline)	I'm feeling better than when I arrived.
Johnella	Could you hold onto this feeling while we explore the circumstances that created the experience of irritation?
Robert (Caroline)	I'll try.
Johnella	Could you tell me if 'the OK feeling' that you are experiencing at the moment is getting smaller or weaker in any way?
Robert (Caroline)	I think so.
Johnella	OK. Can you describe the last time you felt a build up of irritation?
Robert (Caroline)	That's easy. Yesterday. I had all these orders to get out by Christmas, and both of my office support people were away sick. I was running around doing everything and the computer went down. I threw a cup across the room because if I hadn't I'd have thrown the computer. I started to shake and then I felt scared.
Johnella	Can you put words to this fear?
Robert (Caroline)	I thought what if I have a memory now, I won't be able to handle it.
Johnella	Did this thought reduce or increase the fear?
Robert (Caroline)	Increased it. I went to my office and I threw down a couple of drinks.
Johnella	Was there any sign that a past memory was appearing?
Robert (Caroline)	No. I didn't remember anything.
Johnella	So the fear of the memory was present rather than the memory itself?
Robert (Caroline)	Yes. I suppose.
Johnella	OK. Caroline step out of Robert's position.

We could now re-search with Robert the ways he could notice this fear earlier, and then act to support himself by reducing it. It would be useful to further re-search the fear of the memory by wondering, 'If there was a memory what would this mean for your life?

However as you will have noticed, I orientated the interview toward discovering that Robert does have resources - some things have changed - while also discovering his unique circumstances. This is different to an interview in which there is a focus on re-searching an absence - nothing ever changes - then telling Robert what he needs to do about these memories.

The 'I am not' position can refer to small life considerations such as 'I am not confident', or totalising life considerations such as 'I am nothing. I am a waste of space.' The effects on people of inhabiting this 'I am not' position can range from minor discomfit, to hopelessness and frequent suicide attempts. If absence is also at the forefront of therapists' enquiry processes, the result can be all participants collecting copious evidence for the despair or lack position.

Earlier I described how relational language assists us to inhabit a temporary place in which we can explore experience. In contrast, conventional language use invites us to take up a binary, 'I am this,' or 'I am not this.' The definitive nature of everyday language usage can have the effect of encouraging us to take up an absence because we don't feel entitled to take up a place of presence. For example, when someone says, 'You are a very confident person', you will be tempted to remember a time when you did not experience a sense of confidence.

In response to a definitive statement, there is a search for a memory that challenges the definitive statement. When the memory is found, the person may find themselves arguing for absence, that is, 'Ahh. No, I'm not really that confident.' Centralising the relational presence 'the confidence I experienced when ... ,' allows us to explore confidence as a moving, developing, contextually bound process. Through this movement, we can highlight everything and everybody who contributed to the development of a confidence position.

 exercise

I suggest you practice using relational presence by referring to the next diagram. Begin by thinking about a time when you felt a loss of professional confidence; then identify a time when you did experience a degree of confidence. Refer to the diagram and answer each question, constructing a confidence-building knowledge as you go. I suggest you take this knowledge back to the time when you experienced a lack of confidence and ask, 'Given what I now know, what would I do differently to support myself?'

diagram 5: relational presence

What/who contributes to the reducing of this confidence experience?

What/who contributed to the strengthening of this confidence experience?

What is the effect on self, on relationships, on others, when I hold this confidence?

the experience of professional confidence

What is the history of this experience of confidence? Do I feel this degree of confidence now? If this confidence was to strengthen, what would change?

When I act with a sense of confidence, what do I notice or feel?

Which ideas and practices support the building of a sense of confidence in my life?

When we re-search the relational presence position in therapy and super-vision, we may find a knowledge that is fragmented, fleeting or located in dreams that come from observing others' lives. It may be strongly rooted in past relationships, and family knowledge and experience. It may come and go with the advent of unpredictable or traumatic life experiences. Nevertheless, this knowing exists once it is languaged into existence.

We can language experience into existence, for example 'the type of support I need'. This can occur once we position ourselves outside of binary positions such as, 'I am supported,' or 'I'm not supported.' This reconstruction orientates us towards a discovery process that centralises each person's unique and specific experience of support. Through this process of re-searching direct experience, we create and re-create language that closely reflects relationally constructed experience such as, 'the practical kind of support I want from my ex-partner'.

diagram 6: the language of relational presence

absence	presence	relational presence
I feel unsupported by you.	I feel supported.	The type of support I need from you.
You don't consider me.	You do consider me.	The kind of consideration I'm looking for.
I'm not confident.	I am confident.	Have I ever experienced a degree of confidence?
I'm not comfortable.	I am comfortable.	Has there ever been a sense of comfort in ...?
I'm not ambitious.	I am ambitious.	If I was to take up an ambitious attitude, where would I begin?
We don't communicate.	We do communicate.	Has there ever been a degree of communication in the relationship?
We aren't intimate.	We are intimate.	If there was intimacy in this relationship, what would be different?

The new experiential descriptions that we construct are held lightly through the use of relational language such as, 'How does this intellectual trust of others effect the relationship with Todd?' The self or 'I' continues to be positioned in relationship to any new metaphoric representation of experience such as, 'this intellectual trust'. This position helps maintain a sense of movement and exploration. In contrast, the use of conventional language locates trust as personal and definitive for example, 'Do you trust Todd or not?'

▶ example

Jake (client)	I have an obligation to see this through. I do love her, you know.
Johnella	Would you describe this as a love founded on obligation?
Jake	Yes, sort of.
Johnella	How would you describe the sort of obligation which supports the love you feel in this relationship?

CHAPTER 4

the power relation in
super-vision and consultation
relationships

The power relationship in super-vision/consultation is constructed in these ways:

- Institutionally-imposed obligations placed on the super-vision relationship. These obligations require one person (facilitator) to consider and review the other's (therapist's/counsellor's) willingness and ability to practice within ethical bounds.

- The expectation that one person (facilitator) will make her/himself available to meet the needs and requests of the other (therapist/counsellor).

- The expectation that the counsellor/therapist prepares for super-vision by reflecting on the struggles, difficulties, dilemmas, stuck points and successes in the work.

- Perceived and actual difference in the practice-based knowledges held by each person in the super-vision relationship.

- The expectation that the super-vision relationship will create a practice-based learning environment for the development of one person's (therapist's/counsellor's) practice.

The manifestation of the power relation will inevitably vary in accordance with the philosophical premises underpinning each person's counselling model and practice. The relational climate generated in super-vision usually reflects either an objective-observer position or a subjective position.

Whenever the objective-observer position is emphasised in the super-vision/consultation relationship, one person's (the facilitator's) objective knowledge about what is *really* happening in the therapy is given authority as 'true.' The counsellor takes this definitive knowledge back to the therapeutic relationship, where it carries the combined authority of the 'super-visor' and the counsellor.

This contrasts the subjective position which arises from post-modern thought. In this instance, the observer (counsellor/supervisor/facilitator/doctor/teacher/scientist/researcher) is regarded as an integral determiner of meaning through making distinctions, carrying bias and interacting actively with the information that she/he receives (Gergen, 1994. pp 69–72).

Counsellors who hold the position that they are subjective participants, tend to prioritise a process of dialogue that assumes people know - or can find - the knowledge and skills that they need. Through this emphasis, counsellors are attempting to modulate the effect of the power relation by prioritising the knowledge held by people (clients). Harleen Anderson and Susan B. Levin write, 'Each person is the narrator of his or her own story, the expert on his or her life, and the knower of his or her narrative experience.' (1998, p. 48) This emphasis is also a feature of the ways in which Narrative therapists work (White, 1995, 1997).

Throughout the last eighteen years, I have been concerned that the subjective position has obscured the vital contribution that the counsellor makes in maintaining a collaborative therapeutic or super-vision relationship. Inevitably, the people (clients) we meet carry ideas about the role and function of counsellors and therapy. We can challenge dominant constructions of therapy by speaking directly about the construction of the therapeutic relationship. This provides a foundational explanation that can be renegotiated as people (clients) directly experience the effects of participating in the relationship.

Shifting the emphasis to prioritise mutual discovery, negotiation of meaning and narrating in the present moment, requires vigilance from all participants. However I believe the counsellor holds substantial responsibility for maintaining this vigilance.

Consequently, I advocate that counsellors develop the awareness and skills to ongoingly negotiate the meaning that participants make of engaging with a complex, dynamic experiential power relation. Relational consciousness allows me to take up the inside/outside position, which includes considering the other participant's experience of self, other and self/other in relationship. From this position, I generate meaning possibilities that shape an enquiry process that may shift, add to or negate all that I have previously believed (Bird, 2004. pp 181-190).

I believe that the backgrounding of one participant's (counsellor's) contribution to therapeutic conversations has been used in an attempt to 'even up the power relationship' (□Note 17). Unfortunately this has the effect of disguising the inevitable power relation in therapeutic, super-vision/consultation or teaching settings, while at the same time constructing the participants as subjective (□Note 18). The serious consequences of this for super-vision/consultation and for counselling include:

- Obscuring rather than reinventing the boundaries of the super-vision/consultation relationship and the therapeutic relationship. I believe that obscuring these boundaries increases the likelihood that changes to the relationship will remain unnegotiated. This creates a drifting relationship, and the drift is only identified when a problem develops in the relationship. In contrast, a contributor position encourages the counsellor to review the strategies that she/he has in place for protecting the relationship from drifting (□Note 19).

  For example, if the counsellor and the person (client) decide to meet outside the usual context, and the meaning each person ascribes to this change is not negotiated, a potential for misunderstanding is created. When the bounds of the relationship are articulated, we can continue to negotiate the effect of this boundary on the changing relationship such as, the effect on the therapeutic relationship of changing the meeting place for therapy. This could include reviewing the following in super-vision

  · the resources that the counsellor has in place to protect the therapeutic relationship from the development of any misunderstanding about the relationship

  · articulating and negotiating the benefit to the therapeutic relationship of changing the meeting place

- setting up ways to re-search the effect of this change on each person's understanding of the therapeutic relationship, including re-searching any anticipated and actual benefit
- strategies to reflect on and protect the therapeutic relationship from being experienced by either person as special (Bird, 2000. pp 120-122)
- strategies to reflect on any unexpected changes in either person's expectations of this relationship
- using relational languaging to explore experiences as these experiences occur

- In super-vision/consultation, there may be an attempt to even up the power differential by highlighting the counsellor's expertise, competence or experience. In these instances, the counsellor is interviewed in super-vision/consultation around the knowledge that she/he holds with a question like, 'What do you know about finding hope for a relationship when you thought there was limited or no hope?' This type of interview can bring out previously unknown or neglected experiential knowledge, while at the same time moving the counsellor away from generalised detached knowledges.

  Consequently, the counsellor can feel supported to emphasise the specific local experience of individuals, couple or families. I believe that it is beneficial to use a process in super-vision that emphasises the experiential knowledge that the counsellor holds. However it is also important to highlight the skills that the facilitator uses to bring forward this previously discounted knowledge. In this instance, we are privileging the process of *finding* knowledge rather than *constructing* knowledge as static.

  The question that I initially used (above) only becomes meaningful when the facilitator builds on the counsellor's answer, in order to develop a contextual exploration of the counsellor's experience. Obscuring the contribution that the facilitator makes to this exploration creates the possibility that the counsellor will *experience* the experiential knowledge as retrieved in a static form such as, 'I have this knowledge,' rather than, 'I have a method or ideas or skills for finding experiential knowledge with people.'

- It is often very difficult for the client/counsellor/student to speak of any sense of discomfort or difference, as this would be a challenge to the good intentions of the other person. When people sense 'good intentions' coming from a member of the professional classes, their response can be one of gratitude such as, 'This person is really trying to understand. No-one else has ever wanted to know,' or one of care-taking such as, 'This person is really trying. They've got it wrong, but if I tell them they'll be really hurt.' When people find themselves in either of these positions, they are inclined to defer to people's good intentions (therapist's, consultant's, facilitator's), even though these intentions might disadvantage them.

I believe that the challenge to the objective-observer position in which facilitators, super-visors or counsellors know what the other person 'really means', has in some instances produced an other-side of the coin engagement with subjectivity. This position limits conversations in super-vision by

- neglecting the inevitability of a power relation in the super-vision/consultation relationship

- reducing the resources available to negotiate this power relation in super-vision/consultation relationships

- obscuring the contribution that each person makes to the super-vision/consultation relationship

Abandoning the objective position for the other-side of the coin subjective position can result in counsellors' prioritising the view that people are the experts on their lives (Note 20). In order to emphasise this expertise, therapies have developed strategies to limit the effects of the power relation, such as 'taking it back practices' (White, 1997. pp 115).

However I believe referencing only one side of the relationship makes the contribution of the other person (counsellor/facilitator) invisible. Once we acknowledge each person's contribution to the relationship, we can ask, 'How do we relate to and with the complex, fluid, dynamic nature of engaging in relationships in which there is also a power relation?'

There may be many answers to this. However in my practice, I believe the answer to this question lies with the application of relational language-making and the development of relational consciousness.

accountability through relational consciousness

The objective observer position generates a one-way accountability process in which meaning is made of interactions, thoughts and feelings by the professional group. Narrative therapy's response to this is to emphasise 'bottom-up' accountability (White, 1997. pp 200-214). In bottom-up accountability, the consumer group manages the accountability line. The diagram below represents these two positions; 'up-down' in which the professional group manages the accountability line, and 'bottom-up' in which the consumer group manages the accountability line.

diagram 7: up-down and bottom-up accountability positions

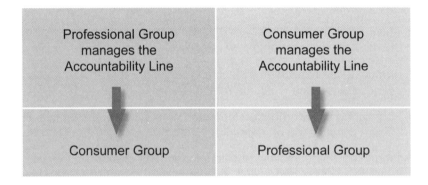

Inevitably, when people position themselves on the 'right' side of this accountability binary, then the other side becomes the 'wrong' side. M. White has challenged the objective observer position, while significantly contributing to the development of practices that shift the power relation in therapeutic contexts.

However when counsellors take up the bottom-up accountability practices that he describes, I have noticed there is limited negotiation of the meaning made of present-moment experience in the therapeutic or super-vision relationship. De-centering has been interpreted by these counsellors as a privileging of the others' experiences, while often disregarding their experiences. This disregard is more likely to occur whenever feelings or experiences are constructed by counsellors as negative, which in turn restricts the counsellor's ability to:

■ Use direct experience as a tentative meaning platform.

- Express, then contextually make sense of initiatives proposed by people (clients). This includes initiatives that would contravene the understanding of the therapeutic relationship. For example, Crystal (client) saying, 'I think I'm in love with you, Rowan (counsellor)' (⬡Note 21).

In contrast, relational consciousness and relational language-making allows me to inhabit an inside/outside position. From this position, I can step beyond oppositions and create another relational place. In this relational place, it is possible for participants in therapeutic and super-vision conversations to negotiate the dynamic and fluid power relation that comes into being as it is experienced and expressed (Bird, 2000. pp 88-139; Bird, 2004. pp 181-195).

The experience that each participant has in the therapeutic relationship is neither 'true' nor 'false'. When experience is expressed conventionally, we are possessed by this expression as in, 'I am in love with you,' or 'You love me.' However the relational expression of experience situates love as contextually shaped as in, 'The love you feel in this relationship.' This form of languaging provides us with a tool to contextually explore experience. Subsequent contextual exploration allows us to find language that closely represents each person's experience, such as 'the type of love that is experienced, as one person speaks what has previously been unspeakable to another'.

The next diagram reflects a perspective that I actively encourage participants in super-vision to use. I invite the counsellor to consider the effects on the therapeutic conversation of her/his participation in this relationship, including

- the decisions that she/he makes with respect to the conversational direction
- what is highlighted and what is backgrounded
- the direct experience of participating in the therapeutic relationship
- the imagined experience of the other participant/s (client/s)
- the possible effects of all of the above on the conversation

Once we notice the experiences we have in therapeutic and super-vision relationships, we are positioned to make sense of these experiences. I believe the discoveries that we subsequently make are more likely to retain a tentative sense when we relationally language them

diagram 8: relational accountability

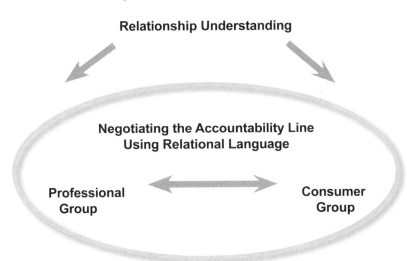

Relationship Understanding

**Negotiating the Accountability Line
Using Relational Language**

**Professional
Group**

**Consumer
Group**

exposing the
operation of power

Exposing the operation of power through super-vision is possible when the experience of the power relation is tentatively named as a relational entity, that is, 'the silence you experienced', 'the difficulty you described', 'the deferring to', 'the sense of being overwhelmed', 'challenging the panic that comes with expectations', 'the experience of these critical ideas which acted to silence', and so on.

The construction of these everyday relational metaphors allows me to contextually explore the experience of the relational self within super-vision. Through using relational language, it is even possible to explore the limitations, strengths and effects of our good intentions. This exploration allows people to consider possibilities beyond the construction, 'I'm right or wrong/good or bad.'

 prismatic dialogue

This consultation process took place between Johnella and Tui in super-vision/consultation (⬛Note 22).

Johnella	This strong feeling which you describe as 'a sense of powerlessness' about the therapeutic work with Meg, when do you notice this coming forward in the work with Meg?
Tui	It's during those times when she seems to be doing nothing to support her life. I mean, I make suggestions around resources and she just never takes them up.
Johnella	What's happening in the therapeutic conversation when you find yourself bringing forward these suggestions ?
Tui	Usually she's saying things like 'I don't know what to do. It's hopeless.'
Johnella	OK. Tui, I want you to take up the position of Meg in answering these questions. Is that OK? I want to explore the place in the therapy where you experience a sense of powerlessness a little more.
Tui	I'll try. I'm not sure if I can do it.
Johnella	Let's give it a try. You can stop the process at any time.
Tui	OK.
Johnella	Meg, if you knew what to do, what would change? What would be being done?
Meg (Tui)	I'd be able to study. I'd leave my boyfriend and get a new flat. I'd tell my family that I need support for a change.
Johnella	That's quite a list of things. When you listen to this list, what are the feelings or thoughts which come forward?
Meg (Tui)	I just feel overwhelmed. I think I can't do it.
Johnella	OK. If you were to pick one thing from this list of things to be done, which one would you pick?
Meg (Tui)	I don't know, which one would you pick?
Johnella	If I picked one, what do you think it would feel like? Would there a be a sense of relief, 'Oh, that's great, she's picked one I can work on,' or a sense of worry or fear, 'Oh. She thinks I can do this and I can't.'
Meg (Tui)	I wouldn't feel relief. I think I'd feel pressure.
Johnella	I'd like to avoid you experiencing any more pressure than the pressure that you are already experiencing. I'd like to suggest that you decide on one of the things to be done. This decision will

	allow us to explore this further. In the exploration, there is absolutely no requirement for this thing to be acted on, outside of this session. Is that OK?
Meg (Tui)	That's great. I think I can do that.
Johnella	Let's stop there, Tui. What did you experience in this conversation as Meg?
Tui	I felt relief. It was as though an enormous weight had been lifted off me.
Johnella	I believe this relationship has been suffering under the weight of expectations! Tui, you have been suffering under the expectation that you must do something. Meg has been suffering under the expectation that 'Tui expects me to do something I can't do.' When the relationship is freed from these expectations, you and Meg are also in a stronger position to re-search 'the experiential.'

Relational consciousness, or taking up the insider/outsider position, allows us to view or consider all sides of a relationship, while also considering the effect of this on the relationship itself. In the example of the super-vision with Tui, the therapeutic relationship was being constructed through unnamed - and thus unspoken - expectations. If this continued, Tui's frustration with Meg could have resulted in descriptions of Meg as 'resistant', 'passive', 'unwilling to help herself' or 'dependent'. When we use these descriptions, we are setting up a power relation that classifies and categorises people (clients).

In the next example, I want to highlight the prevalence of rule-making or the creation of territories in therapeutic practice. When rules are followed as though they reflect the 'truth' without being contextualised, we are creating a fertile environment for imposing power within therapeutic or super-vision/consultation relationships.

I often speak publicly about moments in teaching and clinical work when I have discovered what I don't know through a challenge from people (students/consultees/clients). I have commented that it takes enormous courage to challenge the position of a therapist or teacher.

In one such teaching context, a student reflected on an interaction with a person (client) that she had found difficult. She quickly moved on from the difficulty, and talked about the positive nature of the challenge, saying, 'It's amazing that she would tell me she wasn't happy with the session. I'm really impressed when clients do that.'

When we explored the relational environment, we discovered

- the woman (client) belonged to a privileged group in the community, that is, white upper-middle class

- there was a significant age difference between the therapist (twenty-eight years) and the person (forty-eight years)

- the woman (client) began the session by establishing the agenda for the therapeutic relationship with a set of instructions

- the therapist felt judged, and consequently limited her participation in the conversation.

The counsellor's fixed notion that, 'It's wonderful when (all) people tell us where we are going wrong,' was an uncontexualised truth. Uncontexualised truths prevent us from exploring the dynamic and complex ways in which the power relation is negotiated within each super-vision/consultation and therapeutic relationship. In the example above, the viability of the therapeutic relationship needed to be negotiated.

prismatic dialogue

In this situation, I used prismatic dialogue in asking Iona (counsellor) to take up or represent the position of her much older client (Phillippa) (⬚Note 23).

Phillippa (Iona) I don't find the direction that this conversation is taking very helpful.

Johnella If the conversation was moving in a helpful direction, what would we be talking about?

Phillippa (Iona) We'd be talking about what's relevant to me. This is rather irrelevant.

Johnella What are the topics or issues which hold some relevance for you?

Phillippa (Iona) Look ... I think that this is a mistake. I don't want any feminist telling me I should leave my husband.

Johnella Phillippa, is there a worry about the direction of this conversation? Do you think that I believe that you should leave your husband?

Phillippa (Iona) Well. All you lot are men-hating and I suppose his behaviour is just more evidence of that. I don't

	blame you really. It's despicable what he did, but I can't leave. Everything is tied up in a family trust.
Johnella	OK. There are several important issues here. The first is the idea you hold that 'all you lot are men-hating', and secondly there's this idea that I will take up a position that you must leave. Which one is the most important for us to address?
Phillippa (Iona)	The second one. I am just so confused. You're so young. You don't know what it's like to be in a marriage for twenty-six years and discover this. Really I don't know whether you hate men or not. At this moment, it's more true to say that I hate men. One man in particular.
Johnella	In regard to the decision to leave, I think and believe this is a decision that only you can make. If you ever think that I am leading you or directing the conversation in only one direction, I'd like you to tell me. Could you do that?
Phillippa (Iona)	Yes. I could. As you can see I'm not shy in stating my opinion.
Johnella	If I was to ask you for the details about this injury that Jeff has inflicted on the relationship, would this feel like a siding with leaving?
Phillippa (Iona)	I don't think so. I'm not sure.
Johnella	Could we both remain alert to this because in order to get to know the experiences you're having, I will ask these sorts of questions?

Here I am drawing attention to the dangers inherent in constructing therapeutic models as rule-bound rather than process-bound (Bird, 2003; Hoffman, 1998). In order to enact a collaborative ethic, I attempt to position myself as holding the theoretical and experiential knowledges that I find useful, while being willing to reflect on these knowledges.

In super-vision/consultation relationships, I hope to create conditions that assist counsellors to

- identify the beliefs they hold

- express these beliefs in relational language

- locate and explore these beliefs in context

- reflect on the effect of these beliefs in particular circumstances

Through this process, I am exposing the construction of truths through cultural and gender discourses, while also emphasising the fragmentary and contradictory nature of direct experience.

In the example below, Francis (counsellor) brings the couple work that she is doing with Mark and Susan to super-vision. Mark has expressed a bottom line position, 'I won't move away from the Bay. This is where I belong!' Susan has also expressed a bottom line position, 'I have never belonged here. I've tried for twenty-five years and I want an opportunity to live somewhere else.' These bottom-line positions have resulted in the couple separating, even though they express love for each other.

Francis has attempted to find a compromise position that will support the relationship. She has found the conversations with Mark difficult, as he continues to state and restate the bottom-line position that he has taken. Mark could easily receive the label of 'controlling.' In these instances, counsellors will often either

- take a back seat in the conversation by following the conversational direction taken by Mark

- attempt to direct the conversation in ways that Mark experiences as controlling or siding

 prismatic dialogue

Francis takes up the position of Mark.

Johnella   Mark, you've been listening to what Susan's been saying. She has limited hope, but some hope, and she wants to take the time necessary to move towards 'what's possible.' Is this also something that you are considering?

Mark (Francis)   Yes. I do. But she has to see ... Susan has to see that we are living in the best place possible for us. She has to come along with that. I mean, she wants me. I know what she wants. I know what she needs. She wants me to really consider moving away and giving up my job. I'm fifty-seven years of age now, and I have created this trust in the Bay, and right now I can reap the benefits of it. The children are happy when we can maybe take some time off and travel. I find it really so difficult that she wants to experiment with something that could be risky, because who knows if we are still together in a year.

Johnella Can I just interrupt Mark?

Mark (Francis) No. I'm not finished. Right? This is not all. This is not all. Susan wants me to give up everything I have worked for, everything, just for the sake of experimenting.

Johnella OK. Could I just ask you to hold it there? If we put aside a decision to either move or not move, give up the job here or not, what would we be talking about in this relationship?

Mark (Francis) That's it. We are talking about that.

Johnella So there would be no other concerns that you would have in this relationship?

Mark (Francis) This is where it always comes to a head.

Johnella I know, but if we put this to one side for a second.

Mark (Francis) This is the core issue.

Johnella Yes. It may be the core issue, but what other concerns would there be? If this was put to one side, are there other concerns?

Mark (Francis) I can't put it to one side because this is what it comes down to.

Johnella I'm asking you to consider putting it to one side just for a second. If this was put to one side for some reason, would there be any other concerns in this relationship?

Mark (Francis) What would be the concerns for this relationship? Well, we used to love each other and we were a good team. And I loved Susan's spirit. I loved her independence that she can stand up for herself. And yeah, when you say 'concerns', it is probably more around how we could reap the fruits of our joint efforts. That we and the children could get it easier.

They are suffering. It's more for the children, I think. For me, what I don't want to do - and I can tell you that now Susan - that I don't want to wait a long time for this. I might wait a year for Susan to make up her mind if she wants me or not, or this relationship or not. She has to make up her mind. I can't give her more than a year.

Johnella OK. Can I just go back to this? If we were to put aside the issue of moving or not, when I asked, 'What other concerns were there', you are really

	struggling to find those concerns. In fact, what you remembered, what came to your memory as you put aside moving or not, was the love you have for her. The good team that you have been, that you loved her spirit and independence, those were the things that came to mind. No other concerns, just what you valued or appreciated about her?
Mark (Francis)	I also ... I mean ... You know ... If I'm really honest with you it also would be financially difficult, property wise, to split up. That's another concern.
Johnella	However when we were putting aside, just for a second, putting aside any of those concerns we discovered appreciation. So the issue of where you live, where you belong, this belonging issue, is actually taking away from you these feelings of appreciation for Susan.

At this point, I am trying to discover the aspects of the relationship that become background, even perhaps lost, because of the bottom-line position.

Mark (Francis)	Yeah. Because it's a dominant issue. I only know I can't. You can take the boy out of the Bay, but not the Bay out of the boy.
Johnella	Do you know what that means?
Mark (Francis)	Yes.
Johnella	Do you know that when people say that, they mean that they could be living in Stewart Island but they still feel as though they belong to the Bay?
Mark (Francis)	That's what you think. I wouldn't even go there.
Johnella	I'm not suggesting you would, but I'm using the same expression you're using. That you can take the belonging with you, no matter where you are.
Mark (Francis)	But I need to be physically in the place of belonging.
Johnella	It's interesting, isn't it? When I ask you that question or say 'Do you know where that comes from? you feel I'm saying you should move, you immediately come back with, 'I would never do that.'
Mark (Francis)	Right.
Johnella	Is that right?
Mark (Francis)	Yeah.
Johnella	So how alert are you to this possibility of moving being raised?

Mark (Francis)	Because I know this is the bottom line for Susan.
Johnella	Is that the way the conversations go with Susan? As soon as something is mentioned, does this alertness mean you say, 'You can do that, but that's not for me?'
Mark (Francis)	That's happening.
Johnella	I'm just really curious about what happened here between you and me. I'm wondering whether you felt in any way that I was attempting to trick you into thinking you could move to say, Stewart Island, which let me tell you, I would not be suggesting, but I wonder if it felt like this. Did you feel I was pushing you in one direction?
Mark (Francis)	I know that you are here to help us compromise.
Johnella	I'm just curious about what it felt like. It's interesting, isn't it? I wonder if this happens here, whether it also happens around everything that is said between you and Susan. That she says something and you think, 'Ahh. That's one of those times she's trying to get me to move.'
Mark (Francis)	These are the two issues. Yeah.
Johnella	It's interesting, isn't it?
Mark (Francis)	It isn't possible to reconcile this.
Johnella	I just wonder how possible it is for the two of you to even have a conversation. When I said that to you a moment ago you thought that maybe I was tricking you into something. You responded to this possible trick, and I could have responded in all sorts of ways. Then you respond and then all of a sudden we have ended up in a place that's maybe surprising for both of us. I'm just thinking how easy is it to even entertain possibilities without the worry, 'This is a trick to get me to move.'

I am using the experience in this conversation to reflect on the limitations imposed on conversations of the bottom-line position.

Mark (Francis)	Very difficult. Because that's what it comes down to. Ask her. She's here.
Johnella	Interesting. Have you ever been tricked before into making a decision?
Mark (Francis)	No-one tricks me.
Johnella	You appear alert to being tricked.

| Mark (Francis) | Yes. I mean I have had people try, you know. Several years ago when we came here first I had to build this Trust, and people were back stabbing and so on. But I survived all this, and now I know I have the best team in the world. Even the Trust offered to give me paid leave. Paid leave. So we could just go on a holiday together and let the kids explore, but Susan said, 'No.' |
| Johnella | Can I ask you this question? It's a bit off the topic. If you knew that you had six months to live, and after that six months you were going to die, and the Trust would be what it is, it would go on without you, what would that be like for you? |

I shift direction here, in an attempt to step away from the bottom-line position. I am hoping to create an environment of discovery for Mark through freeing him from holding and reading all interaction through the bottom-line position.

Mark (Francis)	Mmm. A lot of it will go on without me. That's good.
Johnella	That's something you'd want? You'd want this trust to go on.
Mark (Francis)	And it will, because it's set up now. It will function without me.
Johnella	So if you think about this Trust functioning without you, what does that feel like?
Mark (Francis)	Good. It does. Yeah.
Johnella	And if you put words to that feeling, what words would ...
Mark (Francis)	Proud. I'm proud.
Johnella	Would you feel like you done a good job?
Mark (Francis)	I've done a good job. I know that. I'm proud of it.
Johnella	So you could leave through death, with a lot of satisfaction and pride that this trust will carry on.
Mark (Francis)	Yes.
Johnella	In six months if you were to die, you'd feel you'd done the job you needed to do.
Mark (Francis)	In this case, I wouldn't have a choice.
Johnella	No, but it's interesting to me.
Mark (Francis)	What is interesting about it?
Johnella	It's just interesting because I know some people, even if they are given six months to live would feel cheated, would want to stay even if the Trust was going to carry on ...

Mark (Francis)	I would feel cheated because I had to die, but you know, the work I know would carry on.
Johnella	Some people don't believe it will carry on without them.
Mark (Francis)	I know it would.
Johnella	And did you work to make that possible?
Mark (Francis)	Yes.
Johnella	That's amazing.
Mark (Francis)	But I don't want to.
Johnella	I know. I know. I'm not asking you to. I'm just really intrigued that you have made it possible.
Mark (Francis)	I know that. Yeah. And Susan will support that too. It was hard work believe me.
Johnella	I'm sure it was.
Mark (Francis)	And I hold it so dear. I will never at fifty-seven years of age do what Susan wants me to do. We are so different in all aspects now. She wants me to go, maybe live with her in Wellington, get a job and ...
Johnella	When would you know Mark, that your job was done with this Trust?
Mark (Francis)	It's ongoing ... It is ongoing and will be ... I will always have a place there if I stay. If I leave, I won't.
Johnella	As somebody who has worked in this Trust, have you ever had somebody working with you who you felt their job was done?
Mark (Francis)	Yeah. You know, I had quite a turn over initially.
Johnella	Have you ever thought that it would benefit the Trust if somebody, no matter how competent they were, was to loosen the reins a little bit, to step aside a little bit?
Mark (Francis)	I do that now.
Johnella	No. I'm not talking about you. I'm just talking about your experience with somebody else. Have you ever had that?
Mark (Francis)	Yes.
Johnella	How do you tell somebody to do that? That it was time that they loosened the reins?
Mark (Francis)	Well, you know, it's all done in collaboration.
Johnella	How do you know it's time? Like how would you know it's the time for you?
Mark (Francis)	What do you mean?
Johnella	For you, to let the Trust perhaps ...
Mark (Francis)	I want to do that when I'm ninety years old.
Johnella	But what would tell you?

Mark (Francis)	I mean, I could go tomorrow.
Johnella	Yes. But what would tell you? Let's say instead of ninety, it was seventy years, what would tell you to step aside?
Mark (Francis)	You know, this is safe place for me to work. This is a safe income. It might be the same income as ten years ago, but it's a safe income.
Johnella	I'm not suggesting you do what I'm saying ...
Mark (Francis)	That's what I'm getting.
Johnella	I'm saying, what would tell you just like with other people you've worked with? What would tell you at say seventy years, rather than ninety years, that for the Trust's sake it was important for you to start maybe handing over some more of the responsibilities? What would give you that sign?
Mark (Francis)	If I want to sit back.
Johnella	So it's about wanting, which is curious because with other people you've worked with, you noticed, you saw something that told you that it's time for them to start to step aside.
Mark (Francis)	Well, you know, some had to go. They were just useless.
Johnella	Let's say those people you felt it was their time, they needed to move onto other things, what was it that told you that?
Mark (Francis)	Because they got complacent in general. They ran out of energy and enthusiasm, whereas I kept that all those years. That enthusiasm. That energy.
Johnella	Is there anybody in the Trust that could say to you, 'For the Trust's sake, we think you should step aside slightly?'
Mark (Francis)	No. I don't think so. That would not happen because I have been the blood of this.
Johnella	No one else could say this to you? Even lovingly?
Mark (Francis)	They might. They might.
Johnella	Would you hear it if it's said lovingly? I'm just interested.
Francis	Umm. Actually Johnella, I don't know how Mark would answer this.
Johnella	Yeah OK. Can you see where I'm going with this? I can feel the tension in the room. Can you feel the tension in the room?
Francis	Yes. (Laughter) I would never have this conversation in that way because Mark doesn't stop talking.

Johnella	In that case, I'd stop the talk. I'd say,
	I'd like you to stop Mark. Mark, I'm going to do something now and I'd rather you didn't experience this as rude. But given the objectives we've all established together, if I continue to listen it's a bit like I could step into this river of logic - or the river of your ideas - but I think it will just take us in the same direction. So I'm going from time to time to ask you to stop talking. It's not because I think your ideas aren't worthwhile. It's because I need to understand something. That's why I'm stopping the conversation. Now can you let me do this? Because if I misunderstand something we're not going to have a very useful session.'
	Francis, you need to find a way to slow the conversation. I don't know whether the direction we've just talked about is going to be useful. What I'm trying to do here is to re-search those areas of knowledge he has, outside of their intimate relationship. That's why I moved into death, because ...
Francis	It's almost a life and death situation.
Johnella	When I asked those questions, I wanted to find out whether he has any concept of the impermanence of things. Like, you may spend your lifetime creating this wonderful thing and eventually you too will die. Does he have any sense of that?
	Well, it seems he does. So he does have a sort of binary position, which is, 'While I'm living, it stays the same.' By even asking those questions, I'm introducing the possibility, that even while you're living, things may be changing. Energy levels may drop as you become older, for example. You know your vision will be different. Maybe young people have a different vision that might need to be incorporated into the Trust, that sort of thing.
	I'm trying to see how moveable he is. And you can see as you represented him, there's not a lot of movement. I'm raising the possibility which is, if he's the only person that ever determines what's going to happen at the Trust, then he could get to seventy-eight and still think he is running a

	productive Trust, only to find everybody else has gone somewhere else.
Francis	Yeah. This is the way. I need to find out if there's any possibility for any movement.
Johnella	I'm wondering if it's possible to negotiate the movement that occurs in life and in relationships differently. Can he engage with this movement in life circumstances without feeling imposed upon?

When counsellors participate in prismatic dialogue, they experience movement through the development of new conversational directions. The conversational directions we explore may or may not be useful to the actual people (clients) with whom the counsellor is working. However once counsellors are liberated from the stuck position that they are describing (including anxieties like, 'If I say that ... people will get upset'), then they are once again positioned for discovery.

CHAPTER 5

extending the
imaginative resource

I have emphasised the importance of using the imagination in the books 'The Heart's Narrative' (pp 199-202, 235-237) and 'Talk That Sings' (pp 196-204). The 'imaginative resource' to which I am referring includes:

- The use of questions that assist people to consider imaginative possibilities, without committing to these possibilities.

- The counsellor's ability to use relational consciousness by inhabiting the insider/outsider position. This ability helps us to create the language that more readily reflects each person's unique direct experience.

This extension of available language occurs through incorporating the relational and emotional environment within which the words are spoken. In the present moment, the focus shifts from a close-up engagement with the people (clients) in front of me, to a more distant perspective from which I see all the participants in the therapeutic relationship, and all that surrounds this relationship.

In this environment, words move from reflecting a flat two dimensional form into three dimensions. For me, this move is accompanied by visual images. Other three dimensional forms may be available to other counsellors. I hold the three dimensional form as a possible knowledge resource which informs each question that I ask. In return, the answer to the question informs the three dimensional representation. An analogy for this movement might be listening to an orchestra, then moving to listen to one instrument, and back to the orchestra.

I believe that nourishing the imagination is a life-long obligation for counsellors. The imagination can be extended through films, books, music, television, conversation and within super-vision/consultation. Using the process of prismatic dialogue is one way to access the therapist's imaginative resource.

Another method for extending the imaginative resource in super-vision is to work with direct experience. I do this by asking the counsellor to review or summarise a therapeutic situation with which they are working, and then use the following process

- identify a number of key themes
- reconstruct these themes into relational language
- ask the counsellor to pick one of these themes
- if I am working with a single counsellor, interview the counsellor in relation to the relevance of this theme in his/her life *OR*
- if I am working with a group, people interview each other with my assistance
- after the interview, we discuss how the discoveries made could assist the therapy

This super-vision process uses the direct experience of the counsellor to benefit the therapy in these ways:

- The counsellor directly experiences the emotional and cognitive effect of certain questions, lines of enquiry and tones of voice.
- The counsellor directly experiences the amount of detail required to develop a contextual environment in which both people (therapist and client) are making discoveries together.
- The counsellor is closely connected to an insider position throughout the interview. At the end of the interview, the discussion moves people to a less subjective insider/outsider position.
- In group environments in which colleagues interview each other, we have the opportunity to teach and learn experientially.

- After the interview, the counsellor holds a different experiential knowledge which subsequently informs the therapeutic enquiry. This experiential knowledge expands the resources available to the therapist. It doesn't provide answers or solutions.

I use prismatic dialogue, and an exploration of direct experience, to extend the counsellor's imaginative resource. This imaginative resource is the reservoir which nourishes new enquiry possibilities. This is an antithesis to a super-vision/consultation process in which answers are primarily provided by using generalisations produced by the study of professional writings.

the use of the imagination and working with the power relation in super-vision

common questions asked in super-vision

I am presenting these general questions and responses in a didactic format for ease of reading. In super-vision, I prefer to use a prismatic dialogue instead of, or as an adjunct to a general discussion. I do this in order to emphasis the difference between a detached explanation and a subjective, experiential exploration.

Q1 **When I think about participating in prismatic dialogue, I get really nervous because:**

a I'm worried about getting it wrong and misrepresenting the person I'm working with.

When using prismatic dialogue, it is impossible to get anything wrong! When you are representing the person that you are working with, I will ask questions that you have asked. Therefore you will answer from the information you have already obtained. I will also ask questions that you have not asked. In these moments, you can answer the question by drawing on the general experiential knowledge you have of this person's life. You are experientially attempting to stand in another person's shoes.

If you later discover a gap between this imaginative response and the person's actual living experience, this provides an opportunity for exploration and dialogue between you both (counsellor and client). I believe every question that we ask is determined by drawing on an imagined response.

Whenever you notice that you are struggling to answer a question from the position of a person (client), this is an important moment in the prismatic dialogue. It tells me that in the therapeutic work, you have reached the limits of the relational knowledge you hold about the other person.

When we reach this place in the therapy, we can begin to rely on detached and generalised knowledge resources. The person (client) is then vulnerable to an imposition of meaning, in which we determine the problem and present the person with the solution. In contrast, I would suggest using super-vision to experiment with constructing questions. These questions will assist the therapist to re-search the direct experience of the person (client) who is inside the experience.

b **I'm worried I won't know how to answer and so I will appear incompetent.**

When you don't know the answer to a question presented in prismatic dialogue, then you're on the edge of a discovery process. The answer to this question may be important, or even central, to development of your understanding of this person's living experience. Positioning yourself as discovering rather than knowing, will assist you to challenge the notion that not knowing is problematic or wrong.

c **I'm worried that I'll start getting into my stuff. I saw a role play once where the person taking the side of the client just collapsed. It wasn't handled at all well.**

Some people confuse prismatic dialogue with role-plays. This is an understandable confusion. However the difference in the two processes is the use of relational language.

Through the use of relational language, the person who is representing the client is positioned in relationship to key experiential descriptions. When you are being interviewed, you are holding the person's experience in mind. You are also moving into a more subjective experience. The relational enquiry keeps you on the inside/outside boundary line. By using this way of questioning, it is very unlikely that an interviewee will become lost in their personal experiences.

It is however still the responsibility of the interviewer to watch for evidence that the person has stepped into their past memories.

I (interviewer) intervene when I notice the person is expressing a strong emotional response, together with a movement away from coherently representing the other (client).

In these moments, I strongly suggest stopping the interview. Then I will negotiate a process which allows the interviewee to step back from this direct experience. When the interviewee loses her/his way in representing the other (client), the interview will also loose a degree of flow or coherence.

There are implications for the therapy when the interviewee steps into her/his direct experience during a prismatic dialogue. In this instance, the therapy becomes vulnerable either to the therapist assuming a consensus of meaning when there is none, or the therapist avoiding certain topics in order to protect the therapeutic relationship. This is again an important discovery moment in super-vision, rather than a failure or a sign of inadequacy.

When people identify that they are reluctant to begin a prismatic dialogue in consequence of feeling fearful that they could enter into their personal experience, it is an important issue both for super-vision and the therapy. I believe that the therapy will continue to be compromised while counsellors protect themselves and the people with whom they work, from this fear. In these instances, I focus on an exploration of this fear, rather than entering a prismatic dialogue.

d I don't think I'm imaginative enough.

This concern comes up when people are considering imagination in a particular way, for example, using the imagination to write fictional stories or paint or decorate.

When people think that they are unimaginative, I suggest re-searching this idea contextually, because it will most likely have its origins in the person's past. In this re-search process, I hope to draw a distinction between the type of imagination required in some areas of artistic endeavour, and the type of imagination required for prismatic dialogue and for counselling practice in general.

I believe that effective therapy will only occur if the counsellor is able to imaginatively entertain the dilemmas that the person (client) is reflecting on and/or experiencing. This imaginative ability assists us to engage as an audience or as witnesses to events, rather than become subjected to or objective about the events, experiences, memories or feelings.

Q2 I want to be collaborative, but sometimes I feel bull-dozed by people, especially in couple work. They seem so certain they are right and want me to agree with them. I don't agree, but I'm worried that if I say that I don't agree, they will get upset.

This is a common dilemma. When people express strong convictions, other people can feel put in the position where they either agree with the statement, or take a strong stand against it.

I encourage people to re-search and contextualise the statement that has been strongly expressed. Contextualising helps people position themselves in relationship to the belief or statement, rather than feel this statement/belief is integral to their very being. Once we create relational space and contextualise a strong belief, it is more likely that we (therapist and client/s) will see and experience possibilities in other than a binary form such as, 'You are either with me or you're not. You either agree with me or you don't.'

When we work in this way, we centralise the process of discovery. Part of the contextualising process is to consider the effects on others, on the self, and on the relationship, of holding this strong view or position.

An exploration of possibilities is more likely when we identify and centralise the intentions of the other person, for example, 'Are you committed or not?' This question invites people to answer 'Yes,' or 'No.' A dialogue conducted in this manner can background the intentions held by both people. These intentions will inevitably influence both people's expressions.

When we use relational languaging, we can place the concept of commitment in a historical, social and interactional context. Then we are in a better position to negotiate a consensus of meaning with people (clients).

The relational language that we may use includes

• the commitment you have to this relationship
• the commitment you have to parenting effectively
• the commitment you've shown to using respectful responses

When working with couples, it is common for one person to feel driven to interrupt in response to an anxiety such as, 'You (counsellor) are taking the other person's side.'

I believe that the counsellor is 'taking a side' or 'taking a position' when they either ignore this interruption, or focus on the content rather than the process. The anxiety often needs to be directly named and then addressed, by asking the person what they would be looking for or identifying that might indicate that a side had been taken. For some people, taking a side can be indicated when a counsellor does not directly agree with one person or another.

Once we know what constitutes side-taking, we can then contextually re-search this, for example by saying, 'If you thought that today I will be attempting to understand the dilemmas you are experiencing, rather than agreeing or disagreeing with one of you, how would this effect the worry about side-taking?'

When a counsellor thinks or believes that one person is controlling another, it is tempting to use the therapeutic power relation to manage this perceived control.

I prefer to address directly what it is that I am noticing. I take the language that people are using, shift this into relational language, and then explore their direct experiences. People's beliefs, ideas and actions are expressed and placed in context, so we can all consider the effects, the history, the development, and the future implications of this for the relationship, if this was to continue.

Whenever I feel that there is any physical risk to one person in a therapeutic process, I take up the authority given to me within the understanding of the therapeutic relationship to diminish this risk. This might mean asking one person to leave the room for a moment to cool down, taking a break from the therapy in order for people to reconsider their position/s, or raising my voice to interrupt an argument that is becoming increasingly inflamed.

Q4 Sometimes I give my point of view. I think it's useful, but maybe it's an imposition?

Whenever I am tempted to present a point of view, I ask myself, 'Could I turn this into a question rather than a statement?' When

I have asked a question rather than made a statement, I have sometimes discovered information that would have otherwise been unavailable to me and the conversation. However there is no rule stating that therapists should never make statements. I make statements from time to time. I tend to notice those times and reflect on this decision after the session.

Q5 How do I know when I'm imposing around gender, culture or class?

You won't know! The only way to begin to catch taken-for-granted truths or assumptions around gender, culture and class is to ask someone you trust who has competence in this area to review a video or audio-tape of a session in which you're involved.

I have found the biggest challenge to this is moving participants away from the notion that being immersed in a gender, culture or class truth construction somehow reflects badly on one's character.

I prefer to consider that learning what I don't know - and can't know - as a result of my immersion in certain ideas is exciting, challenging, extending and at times, frightening. When we move gender, culture and class assumptions away from a static knowledge base, we are liberated to consider the living practice of culture, class and gender as this relates to our lives.

Q6 There are some things that I feel strongly about. For example, I don't think it's OK for people to have a secretive affair with someone when they are in a committed relationship. How do I deal with my feelings around this when I am working with somebody in this situation?

The values that we believe in, shape the questions that we ask. I believe that we need to be ready to move from this value platform if and when we make discoveries that challenge these values. Consequently, we hold values lightly as we prepare to ask people questions that expose to them, and to us, the effects of living-out these values. In doing this, we are attempting to reveal the shaping of values and beliefs through the contextual environment. Once the influence of the contextual environment is revealed, contradictions and new possibilities become apparent.

Rob, for example, was having a relationship with a woman while remaining in a monogamous relationship. He argued that this wasn't hurting anyone as he still loved his wife. I asked him what would he think or feel if his partner was acting in the same way as him. He responded, 'I would be really distressed if my partner was cheating on me. However I suppose I am cheating on her.' I then asked him what he made of this contradiction. He said, 'It's easier not to think about it.' I responded, 'If you were to think about it, how would that effect the belief that no-one was being hurt?'

You are in danger of imposing meaning on the conversation if you notice that the feelings or beliefs you have around any situation begin to dominate a session. You might find that it is impossible to hold these feelings or beliefs to one side, or to hold them lightly, as you explore this person's unique experience. These feelings or beliefs can affect the way you speak, the tone of your voice, the questions you ask and your physical demeanour. In this instance, people will either argue with the position you've taken up or move into a silence generated as a consequence of the power relation.

Q7 **When I leave super-vision, I sometimes feel that I am stupid or inadequate.**

These feelings need to be fully investigated. You could conduct an inquiry into this feeling outside super-vision with colleagues by using a relational language enquiry, for example, 'This feeling I have that I am stupid occurs whenever you make suggestions.' This investigation will hopefully assist you to place this feeling in context. This includes reflecting on the moment in super-vision when this feeling was first noticed. Was it something that was said? Something that was interrupted? Was it the result of an interaction? Was it the result of something left unsaid?

In placing this feeling in context, it will become apparent where it belongs. Does it belong to the past? For example, have you experienced this feeling before in other power relations? Does it belong within this relationship? Does it belong to the expectations that you hold of yourself? These expectations might include for example, 'the expectation that I should get it right all the time' or the expectations driven by a belief in perfectionism.

Once the context that surrounds this feeling is explored, you can decide how to bring it back to the super-vision relationship. As you think about bringing it back, notice any feelings of fear or anxiety that come up. These feelings also need to be explored using a contextual inquiry.

Another alternative is to raise these feelings directly in super-vision. In doing so, you would expect that the environment within which this feeling arose would be explored. Each person might ask for example, 'What did I do to encourage or support the appearance of this feeling and what could I do or say to limit this or challenge this idea?'

> **Q8** When I started super-vision I had just graduated. I had a lot to learn, and I felt that this was appreciated and acknowledged in super-vision. I believe that my super-vision needs have now changed, but continue to be treated like a student or a beginning counsellor.

Before this is raised in super-vision, I suggest that you consider the changes you would like to make in super-vision. I would encourage you to respond to these questions:

➡ How would I like super-vision to change?

➡ What would I be doing differently? What would the other person be doing differently?

➡ Do I believe that the changes I've made have been appreciated or acknowledged?

➡ How did I hope or imagine the changes I have made would be appreciated or acknowledged by the other person?

➡ Do I believe I have reached another stage of competence? If I do, what is the next step for me in terms of competence?

➡ How can the super-vision process assist me to make this step?

conclusion

In these five chapters, I have attempted to represent a practice that reflects the ethical position I take in counselling and super-vision. I have continued to prioritise the importance of generating a relational consciousness, because it is through this relational consciousness that the power relation remains dynamically negotiable. I have discussed those issues that are particularly pertinent to the super-vision practice in which I engage. There are many other issues that are relevant to the super-vision enterprise that remain outside of the scope of this 'small' book.

I have made and continue to make discoveries through the process of super-vision, rather than through receiving or giving information or wisdom. The moment I stop making discoveries, is the moment I seek super-vision myself. I do this in order to discover what is contributing to the demise of the living, breathing, relational enterprise called super-vision. I hope the ideas represented in these pages contribute to your participation in a super-vision process that is both enlivening and extending.

🗋 notes

🗋 1. I chose to alternate the terms 'counsellor' and 'therapist' in order to interrupt a distinction which I find arbitrary and irrelevant. I also prefer to use the term 'facilitator', rather than 'supervisor'.

🗋 2. I often use the terms 'super-vision' and 'consultation' together, in the phrase 'super-vision/consultation relationship'. I used to prefer the term 'consultation' to describe the type of relationship conventionally referred to as 'supervision'. However I have found consultation continues to be institutionally 'read' as supervision. I have therefore proposed two types of relationship, one of which I call 'super-vision' and one I call 'consultation'. Therapists and employers can then choose which they use. In this book, all of the issues I discuss are relevant to both 'super-vision' and 'consultation'.

There has been considerable discussion about creating a name for an enterprise that uses a collaborative ethic, while one person is institutionally sanctioned to ethically review another's clinical counselling practice (White 1997, Behan 2004). I prefer to describe the practice I use for ethical review as 'prismatic dialogue', 'prismatic consultation' or 'reflective practice'. Regardless of these preferences, the institutional requirement to review the counsellor's/therapist's practice according to ethical principles puts me in the position of providing an 'extra-vision'. I expect that both people in a super-vision/consultation relationship will reflect on ethical matters. However I continue to believe that the person who is responsible for facilitating the super-vision, is responsible for ensuring that therapeutic bounds are known and maintained by the therapist.

3. Refer to S. Friedman (1993) for an introduction to a number of collaboratively inspired approaches.

4. Relational language-making is discussed in considerable detail throughout the book 'Talk That Sings'. For an in-depth discussion refer to Bird (2004) pp 3-42.

5. I prefer to emphasis the relationship we construct in super-vision/consultation. I believe that centralising roles such as supervisor/consultant/supervisee/consultee can distract us from negotiating the myriad of relationship possibilities that we can construct within super-vision/consultation relationships. This has been discussed by Kathie Crocket (2002).

   I write 'super-vision' rather than 'supervision' in order to imply a process which enhances vision. Ming-sum Tsui spoke to this in a plenary presentation at a Supervision Conference in New Zealand (2004). I have used 'super-vision' in this book, even though I am also drawn to the 'extra-vision' as a description of the conversation that takes place. 'Extra-vision' implies a perspective with the potential to reveal or contribute something to the therapeutic or counselling relationship. My decision to use 'super-vision' in this book is shaped by familiarity and convention.

6. This was a development of the Milan group's circular question practice (Selvini-Palazzoli et al, 1980).

7. I believe that during the period of time when we (client and therapist) are actively engaged in therapeutic work, people (clients) have a limited choice when giving permission to be video or audio-taped. A real choice involves permission not being connected to the benefits and potential loss of the therapeutic relationship. A real choice involves being able to go beyond a belief in the good intentions of the therapist, and consider what this permission will mean for people (clients) now and in the future (Bird, 1993).

8. I suggest that people who are interested in the reflecting team process refer to S. Friedman (1995). I give the following instruction to the reflecting team members, 'Choose a significant theme identified in the prismatic consultation process which also reflects an experience in your life. In speaking about this experience, consider how this will be useful to the person (client) and to the therapy.'

   I sometimes decide to support this reflection process by asking participants questions or drawing the threads of a conversation together. I take these actions whenever I think the conversation has drifted away from prioritising the person (client) listening to the conversation. This decision is shaped by the potential for therapist's comments to have devastating effects on people struggling with life threatening constructions of self-worth.

9. The Child, Youth and Family Services is a statutory service operating in New Zealand.

10. The discussion between Raewyn and Libby took place after reviewing a tape-recording in which Raewyn and I engaged in a prismatic dialogue. The transcript of that interview is available in Appendix 1.

11. The language we use to describe experience is considered to be metaphoric. For example, consider the concept of support. Instead of oscillating between the binary, 'I feel supported,' or 'I don't feel supported,' prismatic dialogue allows the counsellor to explore the type of support the person (client) has experienced or wants to negotiate in the therapeutic relationship. This liberates the counsellor from an internalising construct such as, 'You are supportive,' or 'You're not supportive.' (Bird, 2004)

12. The prismatic dialogue or prismatic consultation emphasises the therapeutic relationship within which meaning is negotiated and made. This emphasis requires the counsellor to abandon certainty through the large explanatory categories produced by psychological theories and models. The prismatic dialogue or prismatic consultation moves the counsellor into the experiential as she/he inhabits the inside/outside place by considering, feeling and experiencing the question and the answer. When a counsellor struggles to take up the imagined experiential place of the other, this can indicate a limited experiential knowledge of the other person. This can be a consequence of a conversational process in which the

counsellor is collecting information that fits into known psychological categories. The discovery of this limitation creates an opportunity for the counsellor to reconsider the theoretical ideas and technical skills which are shaping her/his clinical practice.

13. Refer to the Appendices for other transcripts. There are also many examples of prismatic dialogue in the book, 'Talk That Sings'.

14. As we move away from binary positions such as, 'I'm right or wrong, fair or unfair, compassionate or not, respectful - or not', we need to language other positions into existence. I refer to these other positions as experiential metaphors, for example, 'the affair of the mind' or 'the debate style of talking' or 'the ten-year old type of conscience'. (Bird, 2004. pp 75-78)

15. The development and subsequent negotiation of therapeutic boundaries occurs within cultural discourses and practices. I am referring here to those cultural discourses and practices in which I am immersed as a Pakeha New Zealander.

16. In discussing Lev Vygotsky's writing, Lois Holzman and Fred Newman state, 'The structure of speech is not simply the mirror image of the structure of thought. It cannot therefore be placed on thought like clothes on a rack. Thought is restructured as it is transformed into speech.' (2004, pp 77) I have also emphasised this difference (Bird, 2004 pp 36-38).

17. Although Michael White (1997, pp 148-149) introduces the description *co-vision* as an alternative to *supervision*, he warns that this description may obscure the power relation. He references the power relation in respect to its effects on the life of the person (client). However this reference excludes the effect of the power relation on both the relationship itself and the other person in the relationship, that is, the therapist/counsellor in the therapeutic relationship or the supervisor/consultant in the supervisory/ consultant relationship.

18. Conventional use of language entraps us in an individualistic meaning-making process. Whenever there is a power relation, one person's thoughts, feelings, responses and knowledge-sources (including cultural knowledges) are privileged over others. Therapeutic approaches that use social constructionist and post-modern presuppositions have developed strategies to minimise the possibility of the practitioner imposing meaning on another (client). I believe many of these strategies reflect a

reactivity, and thus fail to construct a new dynamic relational culture. The relational culture I am referring to allows for a more fluid power relation, where the positions we take up are exploration points rather than end points. Relational language-making enables me to engage in and with this relational culture.

19. In this review process, I am highlighting the engagement with ethics rather than complying to rules.

20. Narrative therapy's emphasis on the two-way nature of therapeutic conversations is expressed through 'taking it back practices' (White, 1997. p 115). I believe this presents a way to draw attention to the contribution the person (client or therapist) has had on the other (therapist or facilitator). 'Taking it back practices' is one way to create a living collaborative practice. However I believe we need other resources to expose and negotiate the complex experiences generated within therapeutic and super-vision/consultation relationships.

21. People often struggle to language the experiences they have in therapeutic relationships. Descriptions such as *love* or *intimacy* can draw people into a making-sense process that creates unrealistic expectations for the relationship. The way love is expressed in therapeutic relationships, for example, is always subject to the bounds of the understanding of the therapeutic relationship. This understanding includes professional ethical bounds.

22. The conversation with Tui is taken from 'Talk That Sings' (pp 187-188).

23. This conversation with Iona was taken from 'Talk That Sings' (pp 154-155).

references

Anderson, H. and Levin, S. B. (1998). Generative Conversations: A Post-Modern Approach to Conceptualising and Working with Human Systems. In M.E. Hoyt (Ed.) *The Handbook of Constructive Therapies.* San Francisco, California: Jossey-Bass. 46-67.

Behan, C. (2003). Some Ground to Stand On: Narrative Supervision. *Journal of Systemic Therapies 22* (4). 29-42.

Bird, J. (1993). Family Therapy ... What's in a Name? *The Australian and New Zealand Journal of Family Therapy. 14* (2). 81-84.

Bird, J. (2000). *The Heart's Narrative: Therapy and Navigating Life's Contradictions.* New Zealand: Edge Press.

Bird, J. (2004). *Talk That Sings: Therapy in a New Linguistic Key.* New Zealand: Edge Press.

Crocket, K. (2002). Introducing Counsellors to Collaborative Supervision. *The International Journal of Narrative Therapy and Community Work. 4.* 19-24.

Epston, D. (1993). Internalized Other Questioning With Couples: The New Zealand Version. In S. Gilligan and R. Price. (Eds.) *Therapeutic Conversations.* New York: W.W. Norton. 183-189.

Friedman, S. (1993). (Ed.) *The New Language of Change: Constructive Collaboration In Psychotherapy.* New York: Guilford.

Friedman, S. (1995). (Ed.) *The Reflecting Team in Action: Collaborative Practice in Family Therapy.* New York: Guilford.

Gergen, K. (1994). *Realities and Relationships: Soundings in Social Construction.* Cambridge, Massachusetts: Harvard University Press.

Hare-Mustin, R.T. (1994). Discourses in the Mirrored Room: A Postmodern Analysis of Therapy. *Family Process, 33.* 19-35.

Hoffman, L. (1998). Setting Aside the Model in Family Therapy. In M. F. Hoyt (Ed.) *The Handbook of Constructive Therapies.* San Francisco, California: Jossey Bass Inc. 100-115.

Holzman, L., Newman, F. (2004). Power, Authority and Pointless Activity: The Developmental Discourse of Social Therapy. In T. Strong and D. Pare (Eds.) *Furthering Talk: Advances in the Discursive Therapies.* New York: Kluwer Academic/Plenum. 73-86.

Maisel, R., Epston, D., Borden, A. (2004). *Biting the Hand that Starves You: Inspiring Resistance to Anorexia/Bulimia.* New York: W.W. Norton.

Ming-Sum, T. (2005). The Nature, Culture and Future of Supervision. In Beddoe, L., Worrall J., Howard, F. (Eds.). *Weaving Together the Strands of Supervision.* University of Auckland. 25-32.

Roth, S., Chasin, R. (1994). Entering One Another's Worlds of Meaning and Imagination: Dramatic Enactment and Narrative Couple Therapy. In M. F. Hoyt (Ed.) *Constructive Therapies.* New York: Guilford. 189-216.

Selvini-Palazzoli, M., Boscolo, L., Ceechin, G., and Prata, G. (1980). Hypothesizing, Circularity, Neutrality: Three Guidelines for the Conductor of the Session. *Family Process.* 26. 8-13.

Shotter, J. (1990). Social Individuality versus Possessive Individualism: The Sounds of Silence. In Nicholson, L.J. (Ed.) *Deconstructing Social Psychology.* London:Routledge. 155-169.

White, M. (1995). *Re-Authoring Lives: Interviews and Essays.* Australia: Dulwich Centre Publications.

White, M. (1997). *Narratives of Therapists' Lives.* Australia: Dulwich Centre Publications.

APPENDIX 1

extending
experiential knowledge

This interview took place on 28 April 1997. Raewyn (therapist) introduced me to Libby as though Libby was present in the room. Raewyn and Libby were hoping that the prismatic consultation would provide some ideas for them to consider.

Raewyn   This is Libby and she is twenty-three. She is a mother who has come into our parenting programme with her child who is three months old. Her other two children have both been put in care, and she came in because she had a lot of concerns around coping with her own feelings of anger and keeping her daughter safe. It was a really big issue to her that she could keep her child safe. She wanted to be able to parent this child in the way that she hadn't with the others, and to do just ordinary mothering things like to be able to continue breast feeding, learn how to bath and ... all the practical things around having a young baby. To be able to do all of those things and to be able to deal with her own anger, she found was constantly getting in the way between her and her mothering role.

I asked Raewyn to take up the position of Libby and the interview began. Throughout the transcription I use Libby (Raewyn) to indicate that Raewyn is representing her understanding of Libby's thoughts and experiences.

Johnella	Hi Libby, my name is Johnella. I'm just going to spend some time today talking a little bit about the work that you have been doing. It sounds like you have been doing a lot of learning lately around parenting.
Libby (Raewyn)	Yes. I had been in Bethany and they had taught me some stuff, and I wanted to learn some more about how to look after my baby.
Johnella	Where did that desire to learn more come from?
Libby (Raewyn)	Because I had lost my other two children. I wanted to get it right this time.
Johnella	In the learning that you have been doing, have you got an appreciation of how difficult it was for you to get it right before?

Here I pick up Libby's desire 'to get it right' which I decide I need to understand.

Libby (Raewyn)	Just starting to.
Johnella	In the past and now, what has been supporting your parenting?
Libby (Raewyn)	In the past, I wasn't supported in my parenting. I had thought there would be support but there wasn't. I had to manage on my own and I couldn't do it. Now I'm starting to get some support, but I find it's really hard work trying to get it right all the time, and do all the things that the experts tell me to do. I find it confusing because there are a lot of experts, and they tell me different things - so I don't quite know who to believe.
Johnella	How much pressure do you experience around 'getting it right'?
Libby (Raewyn)	Lots of pressure around trying to get it right. Heaps of it.
Johnella	When the pressure to 'get it right' is around, where is the anger? Is the anger around as well, or not around?
Libby (Raewyn)	I'm not sure about that. I will have to think a bit more. No, I don't think the two go together.

Johnella	OK. So when the pressure to 'get it right' is there, what's in your thinking?
Libby (Raewyn)	Umm ... I'm thinking there is a lot of people watching me. There is a heck of a lot riding on this, and I'm thinking a lot of fears around how I didn't get it right before. So I've got to try really hard.
Johnella	Does that thinking that - there is a lot of people watching me, there is a lot riding on this - does that thinking support you, or does that thinking reduce you?
Libby (Raewyn)	It confuses me. So it would reduce me.
Johnella	That thinking - there is a lot of people watching me, there is a lot riding on this - adds to confusion.
Libby (Raewyn)	Yes. Because I've got to get it right and I'm not sure who I've got to listen to or what I've got to do. So it gets very confusing.
Johnella	When this confusion is round, how would I know? What would show me that there was confusion around?
Libby (Raewyn)	I would become slower and slower in what I do. I would find it harder to do the things I have to do. I would go really slow and think about it very carefully, concentrate on every task, and just go really slowly. So you would see I was slow.
Johnella	Is that exhausting?
Libby (Raewyn)	Yes. It is exhausting. I sleep a lot. I am really tired.
Johnella	So this 'getting it right' adds a lot of pressure to parenting. In exploring the effects of getting it right, we have discovered that it generates pressure but not anger. It creates a context of self watching, confusion, slowness and exhaustion.
Libby (Raewyn)	Yes, it does. Yes, it does.
Johnella	The thinking, 'Who do I listen to?' and then thinking about the conflicting advice adds to the pressure. Who do you think you need to listen to?
Libby (Raewyn)	I don't know.
Johnella	Do you think that the people who are giving you advice - sometimes conflicting advice - need to get together to work out who you need to be listening to?
Libby (Raewyn)	I think they do.

Johnella	If they heard this conversation that you and I are having, heard that you are under incredible pressure to get it right, and that this pressure comes from this thinking that, 'There is a lot of people watching. There is a lot riding on this. I've got to get it right. Who do I listen to? There is a lot of conflicting ideas.' If they heard that all of this adds to a sense of confusion and exhaustion, what do you think they would think about the conflicting advice? Do you think they would think they need to get it sorted out?
Libby (Raewyn)	I would think that they would need to get it sorted out, so I only had one voice to listen to.
Johnella	As you are saying that, what's that like? To think that they need to get their act together?
Libby (Raewyn)	Feels a lot more hopeful that they might do that. If feels like a lift.

After summarising the effects on Libby of 'getting it right' and 'the conflicting ideas', Libby responds strongly that she thinks the helpers 'need to get it sorted out so that I have only one voice to listen to.'

In the conversation to this point, we have been researching the activities, thinking and people that support 'getting it right'. In this process, we have discovered influences outside of Libby that impact on 'getting it right'. I then leave this theme and begin to explore Libby's relationship to and with anger.

Johnella	Do you mind if we talk a bit about the anger?
Libby (Raewyn)	That's OK.
Johnella	When is the anger most likely to be present?
Libby (Raewyn)	When my baby cries.
Johnella	Are there times that the baby cries when the anger isn't present?
Libby (Raewyn)	No.
Johnella	Are there certain sorts of cries that bring forward anger more than other cries?
Libby (Raewyn)	Yes. The grizzling cries. Sometimes that's OK. But then the crying goes on and on, and won't stop. That brings anger forward.
Johnella	What's the first sign that anger is coming forward?
Libby (Raewyn)	I don't know. It's out of my experience.

Raewyn, who is speaking as Libby, doesn't know the answer to this question. In order to help Raewyn, I introduce information about crying and anger.

Johnella	One of the first signs, especially around babies - I don't know if you know this - that mothers find on-going crying challenging, one of the first signs that anger is building is thinking along the lines of, 'I wish it would stop. I'm going mad. I just want it to stop.' It is thinking that happens first. I don't know if that happens for you or not.
Libby (Raewyn)	I don't think that happens for me. When the baby is crying I think, 'What's wrong?' Then I go all through my check list. I wonder what I should be doing. Then I think about what people have said to me about leaving babies to cry, about how sometimes babies demand attention. So then I decide what I need to do, is leave the baby to cry - put the baby in time out - but I find I get more angry then.
Johnella	So when you put the baby in 'time out' as you describe it, where do you go?
Libby (Raewyn)	I just go and sit outside a bit. So I don't have to hear it.
Johnella	Does that work?
Libby (Raewyn)	No. It doesn't work.
Johnella	What stops it working?
Libby (Raewyn)	The baby doesn't stop crying. Sooner or later I have to go back.
Johnella	This idea of 'time out', is this part of the conflicting ideas that we have been talking about? There were two ideas you said to me; one was letting the baby cry, and the other was that the baby is telling you something is wrong.
Libby (Raewyn)	Yes. Some people say you need to pick the baby up right away. Others say if you have checked everything - and I have done that, I have fed and changed its' nappies and done everything -then you need to leave the baby to cry because it's being naughty. So then I get stuck - because some people say this and some people say that, and I can't cope with the crying.
Johnella	When you are outside, how long are you outside before you notice the anger?

Libby (Raewyn)	I have to go outside because I am feeling angry. I have to go away. Put the baby down to keep the baby safe - because I am determined to keep the baby safe - and I go away, take time out.
Johnella	In the process of going through the check list, where is the experience of anger in relationship to that? Is anger already there, or is it building? Or is it not there at all?
Libby (Raewyn)	Anger is already there when I go through the check list.

Here I'm attempting to explore the relationship between the baby's crying, and the relationship between the checklist and the anger.

Johnella	Where do you feel this anger? Where do you know it? Where do you see it? Feel it in your body?
Libby (Raewyn)	When I feel stuck, that's when I start to feel angry. I feel it inside. I get churned up inside, because I don't know what to do.
Johnella	Getting stuck. Is that when thoughts like, 'A lot of people are watching me. There is a lot riding on this, so I've got to get it right ... '
Libby (Raewyn)	Then all the different answers go through my mind, and I check them all off and think about them.
Johnella	At that point the anger is there? Already there?
Libby (Raewyn)	Yes.
Johnella	If you were to look at a scale between zero and ten - between extreme anger and no anger, at the point where you are going through your check list - where would you be?
Libby (Raewyn)	Eight.
Johnella	And when the baby first starts to cry, where would you be?
Libby (Raewyn)	Down at a three.
Johnella	As you start going through the check list, does this anger start moving up?
Libby (Raewyn)	Yes. It would do. The further I get through the check list, the further up it would go.
Johnella	As you go through the check list, do you feel a growing sense of desperation?
Libby (Raewyn)	Yes. Sometimes through the check list I find what the baby is crying for. Like baby cries because

	it has got a wet nappy. So that is that. But the further through the check list I get, the more desperate I feel, and the more angry I feel.
Johnella	So desperation feeds anger?
Libby (Raewyn)	Yes.
Johnella	And whenever you get an answer going through the check list, the anger begins to dissipate?
Libby (Raewyn)	Yes. Because I've known what to do.
Johnella	It sounds as if you are saying that desperation is supported by some of these ideas like, 'People are watching me. There is a lot riding on this. I've got to get it right.'
Libby (Raewyn)	Yes. And it is my last chance.
Johnella	Oh boy!
Libby (Raewyn)	There is a lot riding on it for me.

We continue to explore the baby's crying, the checklist, growing desperation and growing anger. I then turn our attention towards what supports desperation.

Johnella	Let's look at the thoughts that support desperation. Is there anything that you can think of that would challenge those words? As you are going through the check list - desperation is rising, anger is rising - is there anything that could support you to challenge those words of desperation?
Libby (Raewyn)	I could ask for help.
Johnella	How would you do that?
Libby (Raewyn)	Depends who is on duty. If someone was on duty that I could actually go down and talk to - even just to say that I am feeling desperate - that swings it around for me.
Johnella	Does it? How does that work?
Libby (Raewyn)	Just through saying it. And having somebody say, I guess stand along side of me, and just calmly say, 'Well. OK. What have you done?' and 'What do we need to do? Do you want to take a break?' or just having somebody there. So it's not all mine.
Johnella	How long are you leaving it before the desperation teams up with the anger? You are starting off at a two or three, then coming to an eight. How long are you leaving it until you speak the desperation?

Libby (Raewyn)	I had been leaving it.
Johnella	Did it get to an eight?
Libby (Raewyn)	Yes. I had been. But recently I started going for some help. When the right person is on. There is a couple of people I can go and talk to. So I have two people now, that if desperation comes along, I'm not stuck any more.
Johnella	When do you think it would be a good time to speak, 'I'm desperate,' in order to diminish it? If we are looking at it zero to eight, when would be a good time to choose to speak in order to reduce the desperation?
Libby (Raewyn)	At the moment, I speak when I know I have to walk away to keep my baby safe. I think it would be useful if I could speak a bit sooner than that, because I think things would be not so far along the track and be easier to sort out.
Johnella	Do you think many new mothers are under this amount of pressure?
Libby (Raewyn)	No. I think I am under a lot more pressure than most of them.
Johnella	Given that, do you think that one of the ideas that could support you to speak desperation or support you in challenging desperation is, 'Look I'm under lots more pressure than most new mothers. And as a result of being under more pressure than most new mothers, one of the ways that I can reduce pressure is to speak my desperation earlier than I would have needed to, if I hadn't been under so much pressure?'
Libby (Raewyn)	Yes.
Johnella	I'm wondering, how much would you say you were working at being a good mother? Would you say you were very diligent? That you are working very hard?
Libby (Raewyn)	Oh yes. Absolutely.
Johnella	Do you ever find yourself attacked by others' criticism for being desperate or angry?
Libby (Raewyn)	Yes. And for the things that I try to do. It is as if I can never get it right.
Johnella	You can never get it right, but you have got to get it right.
Libby (Raewyn)	Yes.
Johnella	That's pretty tough.

Libby (Raewyn)	Everybody has advice on babies. I wrap baby up really warmly. People criticise me because she is too warmly wrapped. If I don't wrap her up warmly and go out, somebody says ... or if I go out too early, or too late ... I never get it right.
Johnella	So you are really suffering under scrutiny?
Libby (Raewyn)	Yes. I am.
Johnella	Thinking about all those things, do you think it's reasonable for you to act earlier than act later in speaking about the desperation? Given that you are under more scrutiny that most new parents are under - lot more pressure than most new parents are - do you think that it may be useful to speak about the desperation faster than you have been?
Libby (Raewyn)	I have to. Just to get out from the situation. Because when I do speak up, the whole situation comes out differently. Better.
Johnella	What we are talking about here is not improving parenting, but finding strategies to deal with the desperation you experience. It seems to me that part of the desperation doesn't belong to you. It belongs to being scrutinised and being looked at, and being given conflicting advice. Do you mind if we finish there?
Libby (Raewyn)	That's fine.

We have been researching the effects on desperation of speaking about the desperation. We are also identifying a way to relate to desperation that challenges criticism by reflecting on the effects of 'having to get it right' and the effects of scrutiny and pressure.

Raewyn (the therapist) then shifts from the position of representing Libby (the client), and a conversation takes place between Raewyn and Johnella about the experience.

Johnella	How was that for you, that conversation?
Raewyn	Until I sat in the chair I hadn't realised the desperation. I liked that as a way of talking about things that lifted it out of an extremely pressured position that Libby was in.

APPENDIX 2

emphasising discovery

During a teaching week in 1996, a participant made an intriguing comment about reading. I asked her if I could interview her around this comment. In this situation, I was exploring circumstances which appeared very different from mine, in that I have always read for pleasure.

Johnella   So you were commenting a little about reading for pleasure, and you said reading for pleasure was not part of your context.

Ella   I need to put it in the context of middle-class school expectations and my children. My children are now adults and rarely read for pleasure. Yet as children they had lots of stories. So reading for pleasure relates to the culture of our family - that I'm not a reader.

Johnella   OK. So what does it mean to be 'not a reader'? What is a 'not a reader'?

Ella   I'm currently staunch about this. I have a preference for direct experience versus reading. But once I know the content, I like reading for pleasure. It's conceptual. I have sought it (reading) in order to gain self-evolution to some degree, for example, cultural exchange, but I still prefer direct experience versus reading about people in a book.

Although I am using Ella's words 'not a reader,' I would now prefer to centralise relational presence rather than an absence, for example, 'If you had been a reader, what would have been different?'

Johnella	In the past, would you say that you would have been 'not a reader'?
Ella	I wasn't born a natural reader. It's like a category. I guess there are people who are born readers, people who like to take refuge in books. Those who learn to read early, inevitably read for pleasure. I guess I get odd periods of pleasure, but it's often coupled with a relationship to a person who is a natural reader. These relationships support my reading, because they've often done the ground work and can suggest books to me.
Johnella	Are there two categories - a 'not a reader' and a 'natural reader'?
Ella	When I read, I really like it. But because it requires a combination of abilities for me, including pushing a pathway through my brain, it requires more effort for me. I have to decode print differently than natural readers. Unless a book is satisfying and meaningful, sifting through the content is too much. It's a cost benefit thing.
Johnella	When you look back at this reading history, has there ever been a time when reading was a pleasure for you?
Ella	Mainly it's been functionally for a purpose. I don't read novels for pleasure. I enjoy functional reading. I don't explore the imaginary realms entered through literature! Normally I'd use other ways to do that.

Already Ella has created a number of distinctions 'a natural reader', 'not a reader', 'functional reading', 'reading for pleasure'. All of these could be explored further.

Johnella	When you had the experience of the pleasure of reading, how did that impact on your experience of reading?
Ella	Mmm ... I think it was too much effort.

Johnella	When you aren't in a relationship with a natural reader, how do you decide to read?
Ella	The book would need to be saying things about the author. I need to be able to relate it to people, for example, easy to love, hard to love.
Johnella	If you were not in a relationship where someone was a natural reader and you happened upon a novel and picked it up, what would you tell yourself?
Ella	With some authors, I fall into their world view. If I happen upon an author I love, then I'll read and continue to read this person's work. If it's too much effort, then I can't be bothered.
Johnella	With that idea about it being too much effort, what would that be saying about the book and about you?
Ella	It might be saying something about different world views.
Johnella	Does the 'too much effort', speak about the author predominately, or you predominately, or both of you?
Ella	It might say something about accessibility.
Johnella	When you find someone who is an easy reader, does that encourage more reading or ...
Ella	What I used to do was read everything that one author wrote. Then I would have had enough. I would have binged and I would be satisfied. This is similar to how I relate to people. I have a few very close friends.
Johnella	When you come across a situation that is too much effort, what impact does that have on reading?
Ella	I don't read those. I think, 'That's a funny way to put a sentence together' and I put it down.
Johnella	In putting this down does that encourage picking up another book?
Ella	I've got a barrier to picking up books. There's a cost to reading books. There's a cost to my relationship with books. It means I'm not having a relationship with other things. I'd have to give up other things.
Johnella	At the same time, it's interesting. I'm hearing you say that if you found reading a book interesting you would read to the end, whereas if the book was too much effort you will put it down saying 'I have a preference to do other things.' So these two things, 'no effort' and 'lots of effort' go together. If somebody

	was watching you during a time when there was not much effort, how do you think other people would describe you as 'a reader'?
Ella	I have a tendency to have an addictive relationship with books - I'd sacrifice other things for them. Now because my life is busy, I just see my reading as one to one and a half hours of disposable time at the end of the day. This is choice time. I can recall times when at traffic lights I'd stop and read. It creates chaos when I'm so addicted to an author.
Johnella	If someone was looking in on or at you, what do you think they might say about you as a reader? Would you think they might be surprised at the view you hold that you are not 'a reader'?
Ella	Oh they'd think, 'She's really into those books.' Yes. I think they'd be surprised by my personal view. I'm very aware now that people's views of me and my view don't match.
Johnella	Given your view of what makes 'a natural reader', what percentage of people would fit the category of natural born readers?
Ella	Middle-class girls would be say forty per cent natural readers, whereas, working-class boys would be one per cent natural readers. There are some groups in population who are bred for it.
Johnella	They're bred for it? The criteria we're talking about for natural born readers, do you think that's a common category?
Ella	Quite common. In the world I live in, being a bad reader is almost an honour. It's important not to be a reader.
Johnella	What would happen to a person who jumped the fence?
Ella	That's a problem. People pity them. Book experience is seen to be second hand experience - waffly and unreal. To think about reclaiming and returning to my roots, I need to go away from the world of the reader. In the culture I'm familiar with, that is working-class, reading is not valued. It doesn't teach anything. It's a waste. It gives people silly ideas that are often disrespectful. It separates you from other people. People are often punished for being a reader.
Johnella	Did you see this in action in your own family?

Ella	Because of my addictive response I've seen it in my father. He read as a defence, escaping into the imaginary. It created inaccessibility and impracticality. That in turn generates a sense of pity and loss, because he hasn't got something else. This was in the 1920's.
Johnella	So during those times when you were involved in reading, what would you experience family members doing to take you away from reading?
Ella	You weren't taken away from reading. They'd say, 'She's got into that,' and it would be thought of as a bit funny. Now they say, 'She started off a bit strange and now look what happened.'
Johnella	So it was a sign of separation? How do you think from your family's point of view, how do you experience that loss changing over time?
Ella	Having lived in Britain where there is a marked working-class, in New Zealand there is one-twentieth of the stigmatization. While the family still acknowledges me, the reading facilitated a passing-over from the working-class to the middle-class.
Johnella	When you think about the change ... how did you see the relationships changing? Or did you see them change?
Ella	There is a pride which I like. It's also impressed others. There are three female cousins now at University. No men. There's also a loss - readers are not as accessible in the same way as other family members.
	In terms of my own experience, there's a cost benefit. The world of ideas and imagination is very interesting. However I feel it pulled me away from everyday relationships. In particular, my nuclear family - mother, dad, brother and sister. My mother believes reading is a terrible thing for young girls. It will rot your womb, so you'll never have children! It's been very bad for me (laughs). I'd never say that, but that underlies the world view. It corrupts you as a wife/mother.
Johnella	Do you think that every time she saw you reading, that's what she was thinking? So when you think about this atmosphere of disapproval, are you amazed that you read at all?

Ella	An absolutely supreme accomplishment because I've been dyslexic, reading was part of my bloody mindedness not to be working-class.
Johnella	Do you experience yourself as straddling both worlds? May I ask the question, 'If you're going back to your roots, would you have preferred direct lived experience?'
Ella	When I was about thirteen years old, I realised the benefit of education. I used to read frantically to improve the quality of my life. There is a social cost to reading; subtle stigmatization, a sense of losing a place in the working-class. 'Doing' versus 'thinking about it'. I think about the middle-class world of ideas and pleasures, and can connect with it because it's more difficult in men's action-based world 'don't think - just do.'
Johnella	In the movement away, when you were thirteen, when you decided, 'I don't want to be a working-class person,' and you took up reading as a way out, you took action in that respect. Do you think at the moment, you have more of an appreciation of the working-class way of seeing the world than you did when you were young?
Ella	I think I'm changing direction, but for different purposes. I'm actively involved in a spiritual life. Rather than reading books, I read and practise. I'm rediscovering the value of doing. It's the same thing as hanging out washing, but it's being used for a different purpose - of reclaiming.
Johnella	I wonder in the reclaiming, is there more appreciation of that working-class life now, than when you were thirteen?
Ella	Umm. More appreciation? I don't think it was so much that. My grandma was a refined working-class woman. Life was suffering and powerlessness, and no decision making. Women weren't valued. She taught me it was going to be a painful life. If I indulged in it, then I'd suffer too.
	However there are different sufferings. I'm well armed with education. I have choices, and I'm not diminished by them because I've claimed my place in society. I can stand beside both groups; the middle and working-class women, and women with power.

Johnella	Your description was being well armed - with choice?
Ella	I didn't want to carry on with participation in sufferings. I have vivid images of the suffering of women at the hands of incompetent men. I couldn't beat them at their own game, so I've become better armed. I've learnt the ropes, so I can have more autonomy.
Johnella	Did you make those choices without knowing where you were going?
Ella	I knew that I needed to be better armed. It was before the women's movement. I just knew, 'I'm not going to do this,' and I started making choices and working hard at school.
Johnella	As we carry on with this conversation, carry on to a concern that lots of schools have, how did you think that you use your knowledge of reading to influence people's ideas of the knowledge of reading?
Ella	I give people lots of choices, and I help them to suss the system.
Johnella	Do you think if young people heard your story in making a decision for a different life, not having a map - or seeing reading as a possible map - if they heard that decision brought loss and separation, if they saw the struggle and experimentation, do you think young people might be encouraged ... ?
Ella	No. But I had a sense that education, school provided a way out. There was a sense of power there. Teachers seemed associated with thought and choice. Reading was extraordinarily difficult at University. I was marginally literate. Partly, reading for pleasure remedied illiteracy. I was fortunate to have good friends. This gave me more power, choice.
Johnella	Do you think there are many stories about working-class people's experience available to children?
Ella	I suppose the biggest thing relates to life experience, like my own experience with my children. They're middle-class. As a mother, I let them gallop around. I didn't require them to focus on homework. Somewhere in my mind there were beliefs that children need their childhoods. The skills can be learnt again at ten or twelve years. They don't need this pressure. We needn't ruin childhood with boring homework. I'm disciplined to think that families will ruin childhood by reading books. As a woman, I'd

	say it's better to read with kids, say two minutes each day, versus twenty minutes of hideous resistance. Little and often and pleasurable, versus doing it. Schools often have beliefs that don't compare to family life.
Johnella	If families knew that young people can decide for a different life for themselves, that there could be a renegotiation of the relationship rather than a cutting off, if people knew there was some loss, do you think it would be easier to consider that one of your children might read?
Ella	I see children making these choices. Unfortunately, no one can tell where this has come from. The family members experience the tension, and feel the movement away by a child as a betrayal.
Johnella	It's very strong language 'betrayal'. I was thinking of language like 'temporary loss'. I'm wondering about how one might be a reader and stay in the family. I'm wondering about the questions we might ask to help families bridge the gap?
Ella	Yes. There are lots of questions. My father went to University, a professional person in a working-class world, first generation. When I looked like one the family would lose, I was like my father - lost from the world.
Johnella	So in this conversation, are you interested in developing questions that explore betrayal, to liberate relationships from the silence of betrayal?
Ella	I think that families believe you lose that person who reads, especially if you don't share the ideas. I see it lots, a sense of longing and loss. If we consider women who can't have children, we can ask the question, 'Do you think that my not having children is negating your choice to have them?' This style of question can be asked in respect to reading. 'Do you think my delving into imagination would ...?'
	The buggers that read, don't do dishes or hang out the washing. Families see kids who prefer to read as 'funny'. Kids can feel betrayed in the family, if they like the world of reading. 'Betrayal' is a very good word. It carries unspoken grief and loss. You don't say you feel shameful. If you said you were betrayed, it implies that you weren't worth as much.

So people, parents, won't say, 'I feel betrayed because she went to University.' They just feel it. That's a heavy number. It requires a lot of awareness and courage to face the pain.

From this interview, I learnt about Ella's experience of the tensions produced when some members of working-class families 'read for pleasure.' This interview demonstrates a way we can engage with co-researching direct experience with people (Maisel et al, 2004). When we use a process of co-research, this limits the possibility that we will impose our ideas, strategies and practices on others.

Edge Press

www.heartsnarrative.cc
edgepress@xtra.co.nz

PO Box 80089
Green Bay
Auckland 0643
New Zealand

ISBN-13: 978-0-473-11446-6
ISBN-10: 0-473-11446-1